# THIS IS
# HOW WE GROW

## Stories & Poems for Perspective Taking

Yvette Prior, Ana Linden, Mahesh Nair,
Sherri Matthews, Trent McDonald, Jeffrey D. Simmons,
Mike F. Martelli, Robbie Cheadle, Lauren Scott,
Miriam Hurdle, Mabel Kwong,
Marsha Ingrao, Cade Prior

# THIS IS HOW WE GROW:

Stories & Poems for Perspective Taking

Ana Linden
Mahesh Nair
Sherri Matthews
Trent McDonald
Jeffrey D. Simmons
Dr. Mike F. Martelli
Robbie Cheadle
Lauren Scott
Miriam Hurdle
Mabel Kwong
Marsha Ingrao
Cade Prior

Yvette Prior, PhD - Contributing Editor

This is how we grow: Stories and poems for perspective taking.
Self-help, nonfiction, memoir, poetry social psychology.
© 2023 Independently Published with Priorhouse Blog

Cover Image ©2023 Janet Webb; Cover design Cade Prior

ISBN: 9798395866240

# THIS IS HOW WE GROW

In memory of Paul Edgar Prior.
Someone who was able to change
and shift perspective, and grow, in his later years.

# THIS IS HOW WE GROW

# CONTENTS

| | | |
|---|---|---|
| 1 | Introduction | 1 |
| 2 | Dragonfly by Ana Linden | 12 |
| 3 | Untangle & Learn by Mahesh Nair | 49 |
| 4 | Made My Day by Sherri Matthews | 59 |
| 5 | Beneath by Trent McDonald | 70 |
| 6 | Ground Zero by Jeffrey D. Simmons | 82 |
| 7 | Caregiver Burnout by Mike F. Martelli | 130 |
| 8 | There's No Return to Sender by Robbie Cheadle | 144 |
| 9 | Numbers Lie by Lauren Scott | 180 |
| 10 | Grateful & Graceful Grandparenting by Miriam Hurdle | 187 |
| 11 | Seeing Through by Yvette Prior | 210 |
| 12 | Winding Road of Writing by Mabel Kwong | 236 |
| 13 | Blogging & Rekindling by Marsha Ingrao | 255 |
| 14 | Right and Wrong by Cade Prior | 279 |
| 15 | Closing | 291 |

THIS IS HOW WE GROW

*An interpersonal process.*

# CHAPTER ONE
## INTRODUCTION

### Personal Stories & Perspective Taking

Stories have allowed people to culturally transmit ideas, beliefs, and behaviors throughout history. The underlying premise of this book is that humans grow by understanding the perspective of someone else.

*Perspective* refers to how we see and think about something as well as what we choose to focus on. Our perspective, or viewpoint, is impacted by mental filters, which infuse and sieve how we make sense of the world. There is a gap between *what is* and what we know or think something is. Learning about how others see the world can help us expand our ability to empathize. One way to attain a deeper understanding is through *perspective-taking*, which refers to actively learning about different viewpoints and how others interpret experiences. Reading first-person narratives, through stories and poems, can expose people to different viewpoints to help broaden perceptiveness.

Our mental filters impact what we pay attention to, how we interpret what we see, and how we categorize. It is important to recognize one's mental filters and thought patterns because sometimes we are limited in thinking because of bias, conditioning, distortions, or tunnel vision. We might have expectations, faulty assumptions, or we might have a limiting egocentric stance where we cannot infer the perspective of another person.

Hamachek (1982) noted that sometimes people assume they see the world through a cognitive window but they might see with a reflective surface. Someone once said that small leaders keep followers small whereas confident leaders edify and exalt others to great heights. The way someone interprets events is filtered through personal projections and those with low self-esteem might be more likely to misread motives of others and might assume the worst with a reflective window. People with in-tact self-esteem tend to have a higher opinion of others and are able to consider alternative interpretations for actions and see others through a window.

The term attribution is used to describe how we give meaning to the actions of self and others. We attribute meaning to behaviors and quite often we make errors as we ascribe meaning. We might quickly assume that others interpret life the way we do, we could be influenced by the obvious, we might only see the negative, or we might have cognitive distortions clouding our opinion. Interpretations are not facts and we need to clarify, identify bias, and learn more about how others attribute meaning to their situations.

2

It takes time to deepen understanding and to see the world from someone else's lens. Individual growth occurs throughout the lifespan and the social relationships we experience connect to our ongoing wellness. A positive quality of life can unfold when we slow down and pay attention to the personal narrative of someone else (Galinsky et al., 2008). Understanding more about what others experience can enhance cognitive empathy. We might not ever fully know what someone else is going through and an empathetic approach starts with the premise of knowing that the world appears different to different people. We develop empathy each time we put aside our own opinions and labels and then try to understand the other person and have concern for their well-being.

Perspective-taking is a crucial part of ongoing personal growth because it augments experiences with other types of learning and communicating. Humans expand outlook when they check their ongoing perspective, which can be done through hearing stories, reading essays and prose, or watching shows that allow sharing of cross-cultural experiences (Massimini & Delle Fave, 2000). Perspective-taking can help humans develop compassion and concern for others because it can introduce them to diverse viewpoints outside of personal experience.

It is important to note that in some cases, perspective-taking might lead to counter-productive, egocentric projections or faulty thinking (Sassenrath, Vorauer, & Hodges, 2022). Trying to take the viewpoint of someone else is an interpersonal process and the context and circumstances will interplay with many variables for each person. Personality traits also play a role and so cultivating empathy is more difficult for some people. The effects of perspective-taking also depend on the situation and relationship between the target and the perspective-taker (Galinsky et al., 2008). It is not a guarantee that perspective-taking, like reading the stories and poems in this book, will enhance empathy, but making time to explore someone else's story can open the curtains to deeper understanding and healthier connecting.

Human empathy consists of both affective and cognitive components and perspective-taking can have many benefits for improved relationships. Foster (2003) noted that to understand literature themes we must read through eyes that are not our own. This idea applies to understanding people in real life too. To understand the experience of others, we must try to see through eyes that are not our own. We should try to understand our filters and then consider the social, personal, emotional, cultural, and generational factors that interplay with how other people are seeing and interpreting the world.

**Chapter by Chapter**

The first story in this book is *Dragonfly*, from author Ana Linden, and she takes us on a life-span journey with reflections about her aunt who was somebody that perceived her as "good enough and worthy of love" just the way she was. We get to know aspects of Ana's upbringing, schooling, and changing perspective as she reflects on her aunt. There are many beautiful extras in *Dragonfly* and it might take a few reads to grasp the layered nuances.

Mahesh Nair contributed two selections. The first, *Confessions of a Social Media Mind,* allows us to flashback with him through the early days of the Internet as he took us from the late 1990s to the 2020s. His unique recollection of the changing digital world allows us to travel back with him as we remember our own experience with advancing technology. The second selection, *Accent is Ak-sent,* transmitted cultural connections and modified assessments as he used humor to warm our hearts. Some folks say that using humor in a story adds a special element for readers because it offers a power lift of lightness, which is what Nair offers.

Sherri Matthews let us feel feline therapy with her first story, *Cat Healer.* We also felt her family change as it moved from the United States back to England, which was reflected in more depth in her second story, *Six Degrees of Separation & Thank You, Todd Fisher.* Sherri shared about celebrity encounters and the many coincidences in life. Many readers might easily relate to the fun celebrity encounters that Sherri describes and her stories offer smiles as we see connections to outlook.

Trent McDonald provided us with action and a bit of a thriller in his fiction *Beneath.* History, family, and expanding insight unfurl as characters connect with more authenticity. Trent's unfolding story reminds us that we do not always know how people feel about us and sometimes it takes time for everyone to clarify and understand viewpoints. We also see how human assumptions can be wrong and Trent cleverly uses fiction to show that a scary life event can lift mental blinders and allow love to permeate one's heart.

Jeffrey D. Simmons gave us 26 poems in *Ground Zero,* which let us feel life's vibrancy as he continues to create the best version of himself. Each poem has a strength and the content lets us understand his grit and ability to keep coping as life brings a myriad of ups and downs. Most of Doc Jeff's poems are even more powerful read aloud; however, the written prose here still lets us feel the cadence of Jeff's life. We feel the material and ethereal appeal as it relates to addiction, race, freedom, and strength to keep going because life is to be valued.

Dr. Mike F. Martelli shared survival tips for coping with caregiver burnout. His chapter provided tips for adaptive coping and optimized function with self-care throughout the caregiving process. He also shared his personal experience as it related to the burdens, responsibilities, and stressors in life while providing details about some of the relationships in his life. Mike's assessment of personality and behavior patterns educates the reader in a way that empowers while it informs.

Robbie Cheadle wrote about her experience with the health challenges of her two children, Michael and Gregory. Throughout the chapter, we can feel what it was like to have so many different doctors, with different approaches, as her family endured 40 medical procedures. Robbie also let us feel resolve as she pointed out small joys, connection with others, and how each new day was a fresh start with hope. Robbie used memoirs and poetry to let us journey with her through the health challenges while reminding us that things do work out and life moves forward.

Lauren Scott brought us engaging fiction followed by author commentary about the topic of weight, labels, and adjusting a critical spirit to becoming more accepting and content with truthful self-talk. Lauren's fiction brings us right there with her character, Keri, as she ponders in front of the mirror. Lauren's chapter reaches a cultural artery as her wisdom reminds us all that we are so much more than outward features and body shape. We humans are so much more than externals as we have "heart, soul, and beauty, inside and out."

Miriam Hurdle let us feel the joy of being a grandparent to two grandchildren. Her story builds from first getting the news of becoming a grandparent to then experiencing the COVID pandemic and coping with travel restrictions. Miriam's chapter depicted the turning points that brought her family together on the same coast and she lets us feel warm details from her personal life. Miriam invites us to smile and celebrate with her.

Yvette Prior, the contributing editor for this book, shared poems and short journal entries that were written while this book was being put together. Her family was in the process of moving across the country and her chapter, *Seeing Through*, captures some of the stress, silver linings, and insights that came once they began to settle into their new home.

Mabel Kwong let us travel along her writing journey as she learned more about maintaining wellness. Her meandering writing path helped her to develop grit and build mental resilience because sometimes taking a step back is what leads to fresh perspective and growth moving forward. Mabel's passion for writing is always inspiring and her chapter allows us to feel the devastation of wanting to quit something she loved - to then coming back around and finding a new approach. The takeaways from her chapter remind us to embrace our unique path, expect side trails, and expect detours and stops.

Marsha Ingrao wrote about her blogging adventures and how it went from an informal business idea to then becoming an enjoyable social adventure. Marsha's chapter lets us feel so many of her life changes with family and friends as she thanked "God for the talents, skills, opportunities, patience, and forgiveness" that have come her way. Marsha's poetry enriched her chapter and interplayed with her shared quotes and personal thoughts about the diverse changes that are a natural part of life.

Cade Prior brought a philosophical approach with his chapter as he wrote about right and wrong and how we humans experience multiple changes in perspective over time. Humans tend to see what they are looking for and Cade explored absolute rights and wrongs, individual rights and wrongs, and the benefit of staying open-minded to expand insight about how we make sense of the world. His chapter specifically came closer to the end of the book because it sums up an important theme here, which is to remind every reader that we might not be as right as we think we are and we need to learn about how we interpret what other people experience.

It takes time to expand outlook and so give it the time it needs.

## How We Grow

Stories and prose can inspire us. Personal essays and poems that are genuine and detailed can uniquely engage the brain, which can then potentially change attitudes, opinions, and behaviors for the better (Zax, 2014). Understanding more about someone's journey can enhance empathy and allow us to feel the intrinsic wonder of being human (Decety, 2005).

- If we imagine what it would feel like to walk in someone else's shoes, then it could lead to deeper understanding.
- If we make the time to really hear, and understand someone's experience and feelings, then it could clear up faulty assumptions and reduce bias.

Perspective-taking involves having a strong sense of personal identity and staying true to your own beliefs while trying to better grasp situations from other perspectives. We try to broaden our perspective so we can authentically perceive another's experience, which can help us to cognitively stretch, radiate, and flourish.

Each author in this book hopes that you enjoy the personal narratives offering unique outlooks and ideas about assumptions and cultural differences and similarities. We hope these stories transmit helpful personal information from one individual to the next because this is, in fact, how we grow.

# Chapter One References

Decety, J. (2005). Perspective taking as the royal avenue to empathy. In B. F. Malle & S. D. Hodges (Eds.), *Other minds: How humans bridge the divide between self and others*. Guilford Press.

Foster, T. C. (2003). *How to read literature like a professor.* Harper.

Galinsky, A. D., Maddux, W. W., Gilin, D., & White, J. B. (2008). Why it pays to get inside the head of your opponent: The differential effects of perspective taking and empathy in negotiations. *Psychological Science, 19*(4), 378-384.

Hamachek, D. E. (1982). *Encounter with others: Interpersonal relationships and you.* Holt, Rinehart, & Winston.

Massimini, F. & Delle Fave, A. (2000) Individual development in a bio-cultural perspective. *American Psychologist.*

Sassenrath, C., Vorauer, J. D., & Hodges, S. D. (2022). The link between perspective-taking and pro-sociality - Not as universal as you might think. *Current opinion in Psychology, 44*, 94-99.

Zak, P. J. (2014). Why the brain loves good storytelling. *Harvard business review, 28*, 1-5.

*Willingly disclosed vulnerability...*

# CHAPTER TWO
## DRAGONFLY
## BY ANA LINDEN

"To-day I saw the dragon-fly
Come from the wells where he did lie.
An inner impulse rent the veil
Of his old husk: from head to tail
Came out clear plates of sapphire mail.
He dried his wings: like gauze they grew;
Thro' crofts and pastures wet with dew
A living flash of light he flew."
   *~ Alfred Lord Tennyson, The Two Voices*

*There is no one-size-fits-all perspective. There is no one-size-fits-all truth. The time, the place, the family in which one is born, as well as their gender, have an undeniable impact on one's evolution and choices, thus making the notion of "equality at birth" quite relative. This doesn't mean a person is exempt from any sort of responsibility, but blame, punishment and exclusion aren't always the best solution either. Trying to take in the bigger picture before judging is anything but easy, often forcing us to face our own limitations. So... how do we know when to reach out and when to walk away? How do we learn when to ask for help and from whom?*

***

"Look what I found resting on my orchids" I captioned the photo I sent my mother right after liberating the small blue dragonfly. I had no idea where it came from or how it managed to circumvent the mosquito net, but there it was, fluttering at my window, awakening this strange feeling inside me. "I set it free, unharmed", I felt the need to add.

"That blue... just like her eyes. She wanted to pay you a visit, I think she misses you." came my mother's reply.
I may not believe that... but I do believe there are subconscious reasons for which we sometimes notice that which we normally ignore. Recently, I've been noticing and appreciating the dragonflies I normally not only ignore, but actually dislike.
She is in my thoughts.

***

She grabbed my hands and pulled me to the middle of the room, a confidence inducing smile on her face. *No fun in being a wallflower*, her blue eyes seemed to say, shadowed by long mascara laden lashes. Meanwhile, my uncle was boasting about his latest bootleg album of some western band; he wasn't supposed to have it, yet he played it defiantly, openly provoking my grandfather,

13

who was choosing to ignore everyone.

My grandmother seemed to disapprove of something, but since I knew I hadn't done anything wrong, I was relaxed.

All that mattered was that rhythm… the rhythm that was supposed to guide my moves, the same it did hers. But I couldn't dance, I whispered.
"Didn't your mother teach you how," she inquired, gently swaying her hands, guiding my little rigid body. I didn't know how to explain that feeling of inadequacy and inferiority that took over me whenever my mother condescendingly talked about dancing and her ballet students… Instead, I shook my head and somehow, she understood.

The look in her eyes changed into something deeper, more complex, which the kindergarten child that I was couldn't begin to comprehend.
"It's easy," she replied in a convincing manner.
*It's easy…* It can convey such different meanings, depending on how it's told. *It's easy* – it's easy, so you must be incompetent not to be able to do it. *It's easy* – explaining it to you is beneath me, you should know how to do it instinctively. Or… *it's easy* – you can do it, you just don't know you can, but I'll help you figure it out.

"A couple of simple steps, that's all you need to know," she continued, helping me forget my self-awareness while focusing on her moves and replicating them as the music was flowing. Suddenly, I was dancing! And it was as fun as I had always dreamed it would be.

Only much later would I become aware of it, but that was the moment when my brain differentiated between dance and ballet. Dance was fun and free, casual and individual, it didn't matter who was looking or what they were thinking. Ballet was the torture of rules, pain, judgement and sacrifice.

At that very moment, she was dance.
"Everyone will love the way you dance. You'll be a heartbreaker, you'll see," she smiled full of hope and confidence.

I was dancing… we were dancing! You dance with the mirror, especially when you learn new steps… Was she my mirror or was I supposed to be hers?

***

"I'm not going to live past 40."
She said it so often, that nobody took her seriously. Her daughter laughed; her mother rolled her eyes with disappointment; her husband didn't even seem to hear her. I found it strange, but what did I know, I was only a child and my opinion didn't matter. She didn't frighten me with that sort of talk; I just took it as a part of her. People were strange and different, they had some funny thoughts, I was starting to learn… and that was simply who she was.

Was it a cry for help? Was she dramatically asking for attention? Was it a warning? In retrospect, it feels both like an accusation and a strong desire… because she didn't die before 40, but not for lack of trying.

\*\*\*

I didn't read those notebooks, I devoured them… several times. I was in awe. I was so envious! But above all, I was flabbergasted. Who was that stranger, the girl between those pages? True enough, there was some resemblance with the woman from my early childhood, but she had been replaced by a mean, narrow-minded, drunken, angry version that I had come to know and accept as my aunt.

I hated writing poetry, so that day I reluctantly did my homework – writing several poems on various topics was not my thing.

"Look through your aunt's notebooks for inspiration," my grandmother suggested. "She was always writing poems when she was your age."

Surely my grandmother was mistaken. Not that insipid, boring, rigid woman… what could she have known about poetry? People who write poetry don't end up that way. But once I finished my homework ordeal, happy enough with what I had created, I gave in and opened those notebooks. The product of my own creativity, of which I was so proud a moment earlier, paled in comparison to what I was reading.

The amazing world of a person I could hardly believe ever existed opened up to me, raw, honest, shockingly beautiful and romantic. I was only in middle school and she was in high school when filling those two notebooks with poems, thoughts, moments, hopes and dreams. But oh, how I envied that girl, how I wished I had that kind of connections, of experiences!

The poems in one of the notebooks, along with some personal thoughts, were the product of the most sensitive, thoughtful, creative soul I had ever encountered in real life up to that point. Later, I understood that she was trying to emulate the styles of some renowned poets, so insecure of her own talent in her attempts to find her voice. But the voice was nevertheless there, loud and clear, full of thought and emotion.

The idea of people hearing my poems mortified me. I was dreading the following day, when I knew the teacher would call on me and I'd have to read them aloud in front of the class. She, however, shared her poetry willingly – it became clear while going through those pages – and her friends appreciated her talent, they loved and respected her writing.

A foreign concept to me, that sort of willingly disclosed vulnerability among young people… Fortunately, I would experience it too, and the promise of such a possibility opened me up, helping me to see and allow it.

I didn't have much patience with poetry at the time, so I read some of the poems, focusing mostly on the diary type entries; then I moved on to the next notebook. That was the real treasure, as far as I was concerned. A memory notebook… Were all teenagers so different back when my aunt was in high school? And if so, what happened to them, how did they become the adults around me? What had gone so terribly wrong? But those were questions for another day and all I could focus on was the connection between her and her class mates, her friends.

Every person who filled a few pages in her memory notebook (yes, a few pages each, I couldn't believe it!) wrote from the heart. Their words painted an amazing young woman I didn't see in my aunt. Everybody admired her intelligence, her beauty, her creativity, her sense of humour, her generosity and empathy. Basically, everything about her charmed and disarmed those who knew her. If there was a flaw she possessed, no one could see it, she was nothing short of perfection from all points of view – perfect grades, perfect looks, perfect taste, perfect behaviour, perfect artist, perfect friend, perfect girl... Even her boyfriend seemed perfect and they were the it couple of their high school.

I took the notebooks to school the following day, to show my best friend. What we had been talking about, the kind of relation we thought should connect all of us, yet didn't believe could be achieved, was actually possible... It wasn't just the stuff of corny TV shows. We kept the memory notebook to ourselves, my friend and I. But the poetry notebook made a surprising splash – everyone who hadn't managed to come up with a poem of their own borrowed one from my aunt.

One last time, her words were given a voice... listened to and appreciated.

Memory notebooks were circulating in our class too, although their format had changed since my aunt's school days. Up to that point, I thought I was too cool to have one. In fact, I often refused to write anything in some of my classmates', pretexting a lack of time. But the truth was, I was guarded, careful not to disclose too much, focused on showing no vulnerability or deep emotion. That notebook, though, belonged to a real person, a well-rounded one, who wasn't afraid to feel or have people know it… because those were people she could count on… or so I thought.

There was something I could no longer deny. I didn't hate everybody, there were persons I liked; and I wanted to remember them decades later, to have a little something left from them at that age. I also wanted them to remember me. I only had one memory notebook, fairly comprehensive for the time, which I was hoping to hold on to over the years. And that I did…

Hers, however, I no longer have… and I wish I did. Her mother admitted to have never read her poetry, or all that childish nonsense, as she called it. Her sister had a vague idea about it, but she never paid attention to it either. Their father was of the belief that children were the mother's business, so he was oblivious to it. What if they did care about their daughter's creativity more than as yet another feather in their parental cap? What if they had read, listened and paid attention?....

***

The room was too cold for my taste, so I quickly crawled into her bed, looking for warmth. She wrapped the duvet around me, giving me a big maternal hug I was still too young to reject.

"So how's school," she wanted to know, holding me tight.

I was in primary school; I was doing very well, yet whenever a grownup asked me that, it sounded more like an accusation than an inquiry. No matter how well I was doing, they would inevitably point out that I could do much better if only I applied myself.

But she sounded like she wanted to know, like she wanted to have a conversation, not only criticize. So I opened my mouth and a deluge of thoughts and fears I didn't even know I wanted to share filled the darkness in my great-grandmother's guest bedroom. I told her everything about school, what I was doing well, what I thought I would never do well enough, even if my grades were perfect, what worried me, what scared me.

She asked questions, she paid attention to my answers and then patiently and affectionately explained why she wanted to know all those things. Even when I couldn't find the right words to explain what I was feeling, she seemed to understand perfectly. She knew what the pressure to be the best does to a child.

I was smart, I was amazing, she said, but not the way others said it – not like I was smart, but I wasn't living up to my potential, because I wasn't focused or hardworking enough. I didn't hear the self-centered "you're smart because you're mine and nothing of mine can be anything but perfect; other people's children are dumb and it's your job to prove me right". Instead, she explained why she saw it that way with evidence from my achievements. She also made a point of convincing me that I didn't need to always be the first to have the right answer, just as I didn't need to be the only one with the right answer.

Competition was good, as long as it was healthy, she made me understand. I was smart, but I wasn't the only smart one. That was a good thing, not a threat, but a chance to learn from and with my peers. That novel notion intrigued me. It had never occurred to me that I intimidated others the same way they intimidated me. I would make mistakes, she also said, everybody did… but that was fine, as long as I learned from them and preferably didn't repeat them.

I wanted to stay awake so badly, just to preserve that sense of security and support. I wanted to keep her awake with me, so she would remain that person, the aunt I adored as a little child, instead of the horrible woman she was most of the time those days. But, inevitably, sleep became heavier than words.

"I wish *you* were *my* daughter," she whispered, kissing me goodnight.

Finally, somebody perceived me as good enough and worthy of love just the way I was. Finally, somebody was saying that not only was I enough, but that I was perfect. That was all I could think of going to sleep that night. I didn't think to pay attention to how my aunt emphasized the "you" in that sentence or to wonder why. She did have a daughter… but all I could think was, how I envied my cousin for having her as a mother… for having a mother who asked the right questions and wanted to hear answers. I didn't think to remember all the criticism… For one night, I let "I wish you were my daughter" wash over me, erasing everything else. The woman next to me was the real her, everything else had been a mistake, a misunderstanding.

But is anyone just the one person?

*** 

"We're going to miss the bus," my grandmother repeated.

First she dragged us out of the house too early, now she was insisting we were making fools of ourselves for the whole village to see. But that impromptu snow fight was too much fun to care about the pouting old lady. The bus was going to be at least half an hour late, as always; we were two minutes away from its stop and the fresh snow was too inviting.

"Look, the bench is gone," she giggled happily and pointed to a spot in the immaculate snow where we knew the bus stop bench to be. She ran there and promptly plopped herself on the frozen, no longer to be seen bench, only to fall on her back in the thick layer of snow. Still and silent for a second, she started to laugh like I had never seen her laugh, uncontrollable, free and happy as a child, moving her arms and legs so as to make a snow angel.

"Get her out of there," my grandmother growled at me while I could no longer control my own laughter.

Between my aunt and my great-grandmother, it had been a terribly fun winter day… for everyone except my grandmother.

I reached out to her, she grabbed my hand and swiftly pulled me in the snow, next to her. I couldn't stop laughing either. Her mother's face turned red.
People were starting to gather for the bus and her grownup daughter and teenage granddaughter were literally lying down in a ditch full of snow, laughing like lunatics, making snow angels. She turned her back on us, refusing to acknowledge our presence before we arrived at my aunt's place.

"I told you not to give her any alcohol", my grandmother reprimanded her own mother when we set down for lunch that day.

But my aunt was no child; she made her own choices, and she had been the one to reach for the wine bottle. I had seen alcoholism up close, I hated drunks, but I was also able to tell what was real in their behaviour and what was alcohol induced.

That day, lying in that ditch, laughing and making snow angels, my aunt was genuinely happy. The happiest I had seen her… I also knew she was only slightly tipsy… and although I quickly chased away the thought, her drinking made sense at that moment.

While her mother and her husband were bickering over which one of them was to blame and which one of them was the victim of my aunt's drunken exploits, as they

always did, none of them tried to understand or change anything. Once they were done insulting each other, they both turned their accusing eyes and blamed her.
She was surrounded by family, but she really had no one. All she had was that pocket size vodka bottle always stashed in her bag and the hope to die before turning 40.

First, I couldn't quite understand it. I was a child, no one told me anything and I had to piece together information I didn't know how to interpret… and she was a woman! Women in families like ours didn't get drunk; that was the men's prerogative. A man could fall flat on his face in a drunken stupor and no one minded it, as long as he kept his job and was a good provider. After all, men needed to relax and have some fun… Any woman who had one too many was a disgrace to her family, a dirty little secret to be swept under the rug, a source of pain, suffering and shame. Women like her didn't need help; they needed punishment and exclusion from respectable social circles.

Then, while she and her mother were having their coffee in the kitchen, my cousin and I snuck to the hallway. My cousin opened her mother's bag and I finally understood – not only was it possible, but it was also happening.

Her dual behaviour suddenly made sense. When sober, she was a bitter, angry, narrow-minded woman. The artistic, generous young woman full of dreams and joy sometimes found the courage to resurface when plied with alcohol. That was also how the damaged woman she had become, the tormented wife, mother and daughter found strength to speak her truth, to stand up to her aggressors and reveal their ugliness and cruelty. But most of the time, alcohol was simply meant to numb the pain of having to be alive, of having to look in the mirror and not recognise the person staring back.

\*\*\*

When the doorbell rings in the middle of the night, the sleepy, annoyed man of the house gets ushered to go see who the impolite uninvited visitor is; the aggravated wife, curlers in her hair, keeps her distance in case of danger. The man looks through the peephole and reassures his wife. No intruder, only an intrusive, unexpected guest.

She stood there, her hair a mess, mascara coloured tears running down her bruised face, landing on the soft white bundle she was holding to her chest. He hit her, she said, so she took her baby, jumped in the first taxi and left. He didn't try to stop her. She was leaving him, she announced.

They were getting a divorce.
The parents exchanged concerned looks. They avoided saying much, letting her talk, vent, calm down. She and the baby needed sleep. They all needed their sleep. Morning found her and her baby girl in her childhood bedroom. It hadn't been two years since she had left that room, that place… for good, she thought. Now, she was back to stay.

It didn't occur to her to ask if she could stay… she just assumed.

Meanwhile, phone calls had been made. Her father took the day off. When their son-in-law knocked on their door that morning, they invited him in and offered him a fresh cup of coffee. After all, they had called and asked him to come. They weren't about to wait and see if he was going to show up of his own volition.

The stern father imparted some of his wisdom, reminding his son-in-law of his obligations, of who they were and the world they lived in. Mistakes had been made. Now they had to be fixed. Quickly, before people started talking.

Then the mother brought in her reluctant daughter, set her down, poured her a cup of coffee as well, and began her part of the lecture.

"People like us don't get divorced," the snivelling lady said, matter-of-factly.

What would people say? How would she show her face in the world? What would they say at her father's work? And their relatives? And the neighbours? She would not become the laughingstock of the neighbourhood; her father wouldn't endanger his promotion like that. Then she took her daughter to the kitchen, leaving the men to look after the baby.
"I told you he wasn't good enough for us, but you married him anyway."

You made your bed, now you lie in it. That was the best her mother could offer. Part of her seemed to gloat, pointing out she had been right. The young man of unsuitable social standing was yet another one of her daughter's mistakes. Yet another disappointment. Yet another failure. Yet another source of shame. She would spend the rest of her daughter's life pointing it out, but none of them knew it then. This would have never happened if she married a doctor or a lawyer. This would have never happened if she had been a good girl, the kind successful, worthy men look to marry.

By noon, the young married couple buried the truth – that they no longer wanted to be married – somewhere deep within their souls. Apologies and promises had been made. Eventually, they took their baby and returned home.

In a late 1970s communist country, to say that divorce was discouraged was an understatement. Most women accepted marital violence as the norm, together with any sort of abuse their husbands hurled at them. Divorce was a stigma that would haunt them for the rest of their lives, socially, economically and politically.

She and her baby would live with her parents for a while, she thought, leaving her husband the previous night. Until she managed to sort everything out, of course… Uncomfortable as that might have made her feel, strained as their relation might have been, she never imagined they would throw her out in such a situation. But her mother didn't want to protect her; her father didn't want to obliterate the man who hurt his daughter. Instead, they made it clear that not only was she unwelcome there, but they wanted nothing to do with her in case she went through with that insanity and got a divorce.

Without their help, she had nothing and no one, no other option but to go back home with her husband. That much she knew. But if she had any hopes and dreams left, that was the day they died.

Her life – the one she wanted for herself – was over. And she was only 20.

***

More than help and advice, she was hoping for a woman's empathy and understanding when she finally mustered the courage to tell her mother. Soft hands to dry her tears, loving arms to hold her and above all, a warm forgiving voice to tell her everything would be fine, that was what she desperately needed.

They would have to tell their parents, they half-heartedly decided. Between the two families, they would find a solution… They both had stay-at-home mothers, perhaps they could help out, if there was nothing to be done about their situation. After all, they were so in love.

They were going to get married eventually, build a family… even if this hadn't been the timeline they had in mind initially, even if they were both planning on going to University first.

He was already pulling away by the time they had to tell their parents, but she was refusing to see it. When you have your entire life planned out and you already found the partner with whom you want to share every moment of it, acknowledging that it was nothing but an ephemeral sand castle is for some the kind of inner death that breaks them beyond recovery.

Over the course of a few weeks, loss and painful revelations crushed her. The life she thought she had was an illusion. The people she thought she had were frightening caricatures of their former selves. The future she thought she had was a chimaera. True love, real partnership, human warmth and support, happiness and good relationships were safely confined to the books she used to love. In reality, the love of your life will lie and use you, will break your heart and leave you when you need them the most.

In real life, your parents may turn out to be monsters that you can't help but love and try to please, in spite of all the rage and hatred with which they filled you... with which they look at you.

There were no kind words or warm hugs. Insults, threats, accusations and a slap over the face replaced them. Then, closed doors and thin walls separated her from her parents... More insults, more accusations, reducing her to nothing. The way her father saw it, her mother's job was to look after the children – if any of them failed or somehow embarrassed the family, she had failed. The way her mother saw it, she had been cursed with ungrateful, unworthy children who made her life a nightmare.

Then her parents talked to his parents... More shaming, more insults, followed by the grim sentence – their boy wanted nothing to do with their daughter. After all, with a slut like that, who can really tell who the father might be...

When two young people got into that sort of trouble, it was always only the girl's fault. Her parents shared that belief. They all agreed that it was in everyone's best interest to keep it a secret and take care of it as quickly and discretely as possible. After all, "taking care of it" was illegal at the time.

In a communist country, where a "benevolent" dictator focused on demographic growth at any individual cost, had banned all contraceptives and women were often seen as no more than breeding machines, people found ways of circumventing the system. In many circles, usually in larger urban areas, great risks were being taken and whispered information was shared between women. In such circles, everyone knew someone who knew someone who knew a doctor willing to take the same great risks, either for money or because they didn't share the communist system's values and that was their way of rebelling. So the mother had her daughter's problem taken care of... like so many other mothers.
Normal life could go on.

But there was no normality to return to, she found... not without him, not without their future together, not with her heart in pieces. She suddenly found herself enveloped into a kind of loneliness she had never thought possible. The love of her life had vanished.

The friends with whom she had shared every thought were keeping their distance, whispering and throwing odd glances at her, who knew why… Perhaps it was their sudden breakup; perhaps it was her constant wallowing; or perhaps word got out somehow, in spite of all secrecy. And every day she went home to parents who were strangers at best, if not enemies, deploying their cruel words to shatter whatever pieces of herself she could put back together.

***

It made no sense. Old high school report cards she left behind were full of perfect grades. She was so creative and talented, evidenced not only by her writing, but also by her painting. I'd occasionally go through her old artwork, admiring her landscapes, still art and sketches alike. Our bookcase was really her bookcase, its shelves heavy with dictionaries, encyclopaedias, grammar books, poetry, philosophy and prose, books she won at all sorts of literary contests, and books she had her parents buy for her. She had read all of them by the time she was 18 or 19. She had plans, she wanted to go to University and study literature… maybe French. Then she'd become a teacher.

So how does someone like that fail to follow her dream? How does she become such a different person? She failed her University Admission Exam, I was told. Fine… but why not try again the following year?
Then I learnt that story, told to me as a cautionary tale. It suddenly made perfect sense.

Their parental duty ended with their children's high school graduation, unless they attended University, her parents believed. That was a big enough honour for the family in order to allow them a few more years of financial support, living at home. Otherwise, their daughters were to get a job or get married right out of high school.

A concession was generously made, though. Her father immediately found her a good, respectable job and she was to live at home for another year, focusing on her studies; then she would take the exam once more. Meanwhile, not a day went by without being reminded she was the loser who brought shame on her family, first with that boy, then by failing her exam. Working fulltime, trying to learn how to do a job she knew nothing about only so she could give her mother most of her salary, being confined to her room for the rest of the time, so she would not repeat past mistakes, was exhausting. She lacked the time, will power and motivation to focus on studying.

In fact, she doubted University was where she belonged… she didn't belong anywhere anymore. Her former friends, all University students, looked down on her, barely exchanging a few words when they met. In a few months, they had become different people. Assuming she did get in, then what? Several more years of living at home, no student life in the dorms for her, that's what. They were going to keep a close eye on her until she got married. Several years of insults and blame…

The prospect made her stomach turn.
Then there were those moments of honesty. She wouldn't pass her exam anyway, no matter how much she

studied… because that wasn't why she failed in the first place. She did study hard enough. But she simply couldn't focus, frozen with anxiety and shame in front of the blank page holding her future.

Never before did that happen to her… but nothing was the way it had been anymore. This was who she was now; another attempt would mean another failure. Her life was no longer hers to shape. The sooner she accepted it, the better. Sure, there were moments of hope and "what if's", but her mother would swiftly bring her back to reality, reminding her why living at home was no longer possible.

By the time of the University Admission Exam the following summer, she was already married to a young man she met at work, whom she barely knew. Her parents didn't like him and she secretly loved that. But they didn't try and stop the wedding, even if he wasn't from the right family and had no higher education… even if it meant they had to give up the potential pride of having a university graduate for a daughter. In fact, they paid for a beautiful wedding, in many ways relieved someone was willing to marry her in spite of her… imperfection.

Perhaps she left her books, her notebooks and all the products of her creative, artistic side behind because she thought she would come back. Or maybe she left behind that entire side of her… and those were mere reminders of an emotional death she wanted to stop mourning.

\*\*\*

"She told mom she wasn't hungry, but mom put a plate of greasy sausage and mashed potatoes in front of her anyway. She didn't eat pork anymore, she said, but mom kept insisting, until she ate it." My mother paused for a second and took another drag from her cigarette. "Then she went to the bathroom and… you know… She still does it."
But I didn't know.
"You mean, the bottle in her bag?"
"No… She threw up. She's bulimic… she's been doing it since we were children."

I'm not sure what surprised me more, that it was common knowledge, a normal fact of life, or that somehow I had no idea about it. But once I heard it, it fit in perfectly. Of course she was…
Her weight went up and down like a yoyo. She went from curvy to obese within a couple of years when I was a child. Then she lost an incredible amount of weight in a very short while. Then, when she started putting on weight again, criticism followed. And so on, up and down, attempts and failure always pointed out.

Sometimes the trigger behind her determination to lose weight was revealed. Like that time, when a handsome man she once knew and loved more than anything showed up at her work… She wanted to greet him, instantly recognizing him, but he didn't see her.
There were people around, of course he had to be professional. But she was secretly happy he hadn't seen her, she was heavier than ever. She found out when his next visit would take place and she was determined to look right by then.

She came up with an insane diet and exercise regimen, which yielded quick and impressive results. He was there looking for her, she was certain; the professional reasons were a cover up. He had finally come to his senses, found her and devised a clever plan to accidentally meet. After all, they were both married... and the male ego is such a fragile thing, it doesn't take rejection well.

My cousin and I exchanged amused glances when she went on like that. *Has she finally flipped*, I wondered. *Yeah*, my cousin nodded.

Attempts to regain control of her life, feeble or not, budding hope for something better, meant losing weight. Utter resignation was putting on weight. Sometimes all it took was a man looking at her like she was still a desirable woman, even if that man was her husband. I still remember that one time my cousin was so happy her parents had finally shared a bed for a night, hoping they might find their way back to each other, so she could live in a happy home.

She needed to know she was worthy. And she needed that knowledge to come from outside, to be mirrored back to her by someone else, in order to believe it was real.

***

All the hard work in the world didn't make a difference if her body didn't look right. And look at her, she didn't have a ballerina's body. Her legs weren't long enough, she wasn't slender enough and she was surely going to have an hourglass figure, her ballet teacher pointed out. Ballet lessons were a waste of time if she was never going to be a ballerina. So what if she loved to dance? Her leotards and ballet slippers were given to her younger sister, the one with the promising body. Instead, she would have to focus on her schoolwork and leave ballet to those with the talent and the body for it. "That should have been my life."

The resentment in her words was palpable. Constantly being told one's sister was the beautiful one, the successful one, the good one, the helpful one, can leave indelible marks on one's soul and character. Neither one of them was aware, but their mother was using the same words to put both of them down, thus insuring her daughters' attention and need for approval.

"Do you think she would have been given a chance if I hadn't quit ballet? That's what put her in boarding school, away from them, with all the freedom she wanted. That's how she got a job away from here, so she wouldn't have to take care of mom. That's what took her all over the world. That's what brought her everything she has."

She was sick and tired of hearing about her ungrateful sister. Everything she ever dreamt of, her sister had. It was just offered to her. Independence, exquisite parties and glamorous friends, successful handsome men catering to her every whim… Her sister travelled the world in a time when people in their country barely dared to dream of leaving it. Then, as though that wasn't enough for her, she became a teacher… Did her sister have to live all her dreams?

Her sister could do no wrong, it seemed, being handsomely rewarded where she had to pay dearly. When her sister had a child out of wedlock and showed no interest in getting married, her parents decided they would take in and raise her child. And that child... She had a daughter, then her sister had to have a better one, of course...

But she didn't know how much her sister envied her, how much she wanted to also be allowed to live at home, with her parents, instead of feeling unwanted. She didn't know about the dark side of a glamorous life. She didn't know there was no such thing as complete independence and that a semblance of it implied countless compromises. She didn't know what it meant to be a single mother in a communist country.

To her, the sister was a rule breaker who was always rewarded and never suffered any consequences. Her sister did everything under her own terms. Envy, hatred and resentment merged into anger. Even when she decided she'd had enough fun and was time to get married, she found a husband from one of the most beautiful and romantic countries in the world and moved there with him, of course... abandoning her once more, alone in her misery.

Her life would have been entirely different, had her sister made different decisions. If she hadn't left for boarding school, she would have had an ally against her mother. If she hadn't taken a job in a different town, all the parental pressure and attention wouldn't have fallen entirely on her. Her sister could have chosen to get married and have a normal family, and the two of them could have shared the pain and disappointment of that experience. Instead, her sister had no idea and kept partying, enjoying her freedom, calling it art, pretending it was work. Sometimes, when blame is all you know, eventually all you're going to do is blame.

***

"She only has two skirts, did you notice?"
The mother's voice was a strange blend of outrage and satisfaction while wrapping her daughter's birthday present – a new skirt. A gift was never a just gift with her, but an opportunity to point out the recipient's shortcomings and misguided choices, as well as her own generosity and attention. She complemented herself on that tasteful choice while smoothing the quality fabric, the likes of which her daughter would never buy for herself… I doubted her daughter would ever wear the ugly, outdated, two sizes too large skirt ("she always puts on weight, you know"). But I kept it to myself.
A mother choosing to prioritise her daughter's education and comfort over her own personal needs, wardrobe and social interactions was beyond her power of comprehension.

The democratic '90s were proving to be a tough transition period for many and in spite of all their issues, she and her husband had always been in agreement on one particular matter. Their daughter's education was their priority and no sacrifice was too big. They both had stable jobs, which was a blessing at the time. So if necessary, they had no problem giving up holidays, new clothes or some creature comforts, so their daughter could have everything she needed.

But the old lady folding an ugly woollen skirt couldn't quite see how or why a woman would choose to occasionally colour her hair at home or allow her teenage daughter to have more and nicer outfits then she did, not to mention why she would spend most of her income on private tutors, in order to ensure her child's future educational options.

As far as she was concerned, it was entirely the girl's duty to have perfect grades and eventually graduate from University.

She could be quite stubborn when she set her mind on something. She was also unflinching in her vision on life, family and future, warped as it may have often been. As so many other parents, she was determined to offer her daughter an entirely different life than the one she was leading, the future she had perhaps envisioned for herself... at any cost.

The only way she could see that happening was to prevent her child from making any of the mistakes she had a chance to make. Once her daughter was on the right track, she had to make sure nothing distracted her. Even a free spirit can become a warden. And wardens sometimes see themselves as well-meaning, know-it-all saviours.

"If my daughter likes a boy, she will only be allowed to

date him if I think he's right for her, and only when she's old enough. I'll be the one to choose her future husband. Had I listened to my mother, I wouldn't have ended up this way. Young women don't think with their brain and have no idea who's right for them. It's a mother's duty to decide, and mine should have stopped me from getting married."

My admitting to being friends with a boy had triggered an unexpected, endless tirade; so I was just sitting there, at the kitchen table, examining my too short skirt, too high heels and obviously trampy pantyhose, as it had just been pointed out to me. My cousin giggled, sitting next to me – yes, she was for real, and it was terribly fun when her mother directed her lectures at someone else but her. Especially since I used to be that daunting example of perpetual perfection… I was on the path to self-destruction, I was informed; boys and ill-chosen friendships would ruin me. Well, at least I was wearing the right shoes for it, I whispered.

She didn't want her daughter to face the kind of decision she had to make or the pain of a broken heart… or to marry the wrong man. So she didn't allow her to date or even consider having a boyfriend. She didn't want her daughter to know how it feels to lose a friend, so she didn't allow her to experience the miracle of adolescent friendship. She wanted to ensure her daughter's access to education, so she turned learning into torture and support into never-ending pressure to succeed. A once active, athletic, inquisitive, sociable child was instantly turned into a lonely, frustrated, insecure, angry adolescent… because mother knows best.

She would have gladly done the same to me, because in her twisted way, she wanted me to have a good life too. She blamed her mother for not being stricter and she blamed her sister for adopting an inappropriate parenting style. Body shaming and slut shaming were harsh truths that needed to be said in order to keep young women on the right path.

However, freedom of speech was allowed... Her daughter could say whatever she pleased, could address her however she wanted and both of them yelled cruel words when arguing. She didn't seem to care, as long as her daughter only did as she was told.
Freedom of action was not an acceptable option for a girl.

***

One way or another, the conclusion was always the same. She was letting herself go. For someone who truly believed that a woman's appeal lies solely in her looks, her cooking and her housekeeping skills, that behaviour was unacceptable. Sure, she was an impeccable cook and baker, but she was falling short in all other respects. And that was why her life was in shambles.

"How many clothes does she need anyway," I wondered. Yes, her wardrobe was not a glamorous or even contemporary one, and I couldn't help wondering how she once could have been the fashionable young woman I hardly recognized in her high school photos. But the truth was, she had everything she needed. She mixed and matched and somehow, even if I didn't like them, her outfits suited who and how she was at that point in time.

A part of her must have seen her former attachment to fashion as contributing means to her unhappy end. But you never really knew what you were going to get with her. She was also the person who took her daughter to the seamstress to get a special dress made for every school dance. She was also the person who collected fashion magazines for documentation and smiled happily whenever her daughter decided to get a new trendy pair of jeans. The truth was, her body image issues were getting the better of her, and she often projected them on others in mean, offensive, judgmental ways.

The truth also was, she hardly went out anymore, except for work and quick trips to the market. Her daughter was a daddy's girl, so they went shopping together – one less item on her to-do list. So, much like her high school outfits, her high school friends came as a shock to me… because I didn't know her to have one friend in her adult, married life. No one to visit, no one to talk to, no one to listen to her or offer advice…

Other than some friendly acquaintances at work, with whom she exchanged recipes, bits of gossip and tips about good affordable hairdressers and makeup, there was no one else. No one else but her immediate family… a toxic trap and a burden she never had the courage to escape.

The idea of travelling to a different part of the country for a few days to see her sister get married turned out to be an infuriating notion. There was nothing about that marriage she approved of, she angrily told her sister.

There was nothing about that marriage she didn't envy either, but to that she didn't directly admit.

One way or another, her prediction came true. She and her sister would never be able to overcome that particular obstacle and whatever was left of their relationship was reduced to cold bitter resentment. Much like her former friends, her sister was abandoning her, interested solely in her own happiness.

Traveling, adventure, love, friendship and contentment were no longer part of a reality accessible to her. They were merely the stuff of books she still read... books that no longer fed her soul, no longer filled her with hope. And creativity was for people who still had love and adventure in their lives....

***

The first attempt was so little and vaguely discussed, that it was easy to believe it never happened. Something stupid one does when one has too much to drink... besides, she would have succeeded, had she really meant it. Perhaps that was the truth. Or perhaps one has too much to drink when one needs the courage to do something one wouldn't dare to do when sober.

The second attempt was paid even less attention. A mistake, the act of an aging, careless, forgetful person, who has too much to drink. Who can really tell how many such mistakes may have been before, after and in-between... Who can really tell if the frame containing these stories wasn't in itself such an attempt – the successful one.

Forty wasn't her scary age, not really, it eventually

became clear. Forty was the age which would have allowed her to see her daughter as a university student and take in the experience for a while. Perhaps forty was also the age that would prevent her from seeing her daughter as an unhappy and disillusioned mature woman. "Alive" was her scary age.

But whether she liked it or not, whether she wanted it or not, she had a duty as a mother; and twenty was the age a young woman could be trusted to make her own decisions, to handle life and keep following that right path a mother has chosen for her. That's why she only wanted to make it to 40.

But death doesn't come on schedule, when you call it, no matter how loud you scream. Death needs convincing, regardless of whether you want it to come or you want it to stay away.

It can be a decade-long process, no matter how hard you work at speeding it up, drink after drink, after pointless depressing drink. And sometimes, when you're so close you can peek through the crack of that opening door, a hand pulls you back, holds you here, too strong for you to fight it.

Her liver was in such a bad state when her sister almost forcefully took her to the hospital, that the doctor only gave her a few more months to live.

She had systematically refused any sort of medical treatment, no matter who suggested it, finally seeing her wish come true. She may not have had the courage of a quick, decisive gesture, but she had the determination to let herself die, even slowly and painfully. Yet, her sister's unexpected arrival and her pushy ways threw her, making her unable to resist, ashamed of her condition.

If she quit drinking, if she followed treatment and a healthy diet, she might still have a chance, the doctor said. But a chance for what? That was the silent question over the final years of her life.

"She asked for a few cigarettes in the taxi, when I took her home. She had no money. So I gave her my pack and whatever cash I had on me. Do you think I shouldn't have done that, do you think she'll go and buy booze?" I knew what my mother needed to hear. But it didn't really matter what I thought or what the money was for, because if she really wanted to drink, she could find a way. What mattered was that for once, the sisters were having an honest, warm moment. When one of them had taken the other to the hospital a few years back, it wasn't so much out of generosity, but out of a need to be the hero, the one who outshines the other, the one who saves the day and then returns to her own existence, feeling good about herself.

This time, however, the connection was real and for a few moments, they could see past old rivalries, blame and frustration. For a few moments, each of them had a sister.

Since death had once again been postponed, she gave living another try. She gave leaving her husband another try. Their daughter was old enough and had a life of her own; and no one cared about her marital status anymore. Once again, their financial situation came into question and she found herself with even fewer means than when she was a newlywed. Once again, she asked for help. Once again, the answer was *no*.

"You should have let me die when I had the chance," she pointed out to her sister.

She needed so much more than to not be allowed to die... so much more that no one could offer her... that she certainly couldn't offer herself.

She wouldn't allow anyone to distract her from her path again.

***

Beautiful and ugly, delicate and strong, graceful and maladroit, dragonflies seem to be a paradox of antagonistic features, much like the antithetical feelings and superstitions they awaken. Nevertheless, whether they're the embodiment of good luck or misfortune's omen, they rarely go unnoticed.

*Dragonfly* was my aunt's middle name. Little did her parents know it would encompass her identity far better than the first name they had chosen for her.

The last time I saw her was at a funeral. She was so small and frail, that I was afraid I would hurt her if I hugged her too tightly. But her enormous blue eyes smiled at me, sincerely happy to see me one more time. That time, the only time she saw me as a mature woman, she was proud of the person I had become. She'd been wrong about my future and she was happy for me.

Words weren't really necessary, not with those eyes of hers… those eyes that were sad even when she was happy.

"You know how she was telling me you were the daughter she always wanted and I was so lucky to have you…" my mother added, thanking me for that photo of a dragonfly resting on an orchid.

A Dragonfly will put you down and try to control you, thinking that's the only way she can help. But that's not all she will do.

A Dragonfly will bake you a birthday cake when she fears no one else will.

A Dragonfly will teach you how to dance through life.

A Dragonfly will teach you confidence.

A Dragonfly will fly... and she will crash.

A Dragonfly will lose her way, get tangled up behind a mosquito net and she will need help finding her way back to freedom.

A blue-eyed Dragonfly will wear a burgundy coat at a funeral where everyone is wearing black.

Happy peaceful flight, Dragonfly!

© Ana Linden 2022

*Appreciate little moments...*

# CHAPTER THREE
## UNTANGLE & LEARN
## BY MAHESH NAIR

For my chapter, I have two stories, 'Confessions Of A Social Media Mind' and 'Accent is Ak-sent,' which, though unrelated, have shaped my perspective of life and people in more ways than I imagined. In both nonfiction narratives, be it the evolution and corruption of social media or how an accent isn't as fake as a biased opinion, I have seen myself unentangle, learn, grow, and appreciate little moments. These little moments and events tend to be overlooked and even undervalued, like a friend lending you money without thinking or a plumber leaving a lasting impression. Still, they are as valuable, and impactful, to life as the drops of water forming the ocean. The key is to recognize them timely.

\*\*\*

## Confessions Of A Social Media Mind

Some rules thrived in our home in Delhi. Boys were allowed to visit if they belonged to good families. Girls could be friends as long as they maintained a physical distance. Our childhood mirrored pensive sadness.

As a teenager in the mid-90s, I was a victim of my previous generation's regressive outlook, which had shown no signs of letting up. Their regression wasn't a calculated demeanor, as they were decoding the world themselves. But their puerile conduct subdued me, and my superficial layers remained unpeeled due to limited social interactions. In hindsight, I wonder if their over-protectiveness was my life vest in unpredictable waters.

Then came the dial-up connection and the world wide web, like sips of water to someone delirious from thirst. With an email account on Yahoo in 2001, signing up on Yahoo Messenger was easy.

Soon I was in several group chat rooms, where I mocked other countries because their teams beat India in cricket matches, befriended strange people because they pinged me first, and became a woman myself to fool curious men.

A mighty resurgence kept me going, mitigating my melancholy. A deterrent, however, was the eldritch sound the dial-up made in the middle of the night, waking up parents in the other room. But they soon adapted and kept quiet, preventing my rebellious bubbles from bursting. And I was addicted to black coffee.

AOL had acquired Instant Messaging Client or ICQ, a simple program that made abusing or flirting user-friendly without pop-ups.

My stint with MSN Messenger was brief. I used it to chide a friend who had an account.

Soon I was making friends from Honolulu in Hawaii to as near as Vasant Kunj in Delhi. The fiery virtual life made me assertive, and though I was meeting friends in the real world, what felt more comforting were the anonymity and ubiquitousness of the online world. I chose to save my day's frustration for the evenings, post the howl of the dial-up.

A friend suggested Orkut, a social networking site that cleverly replaced our limited real meetings. The friends were thrilled, sharing their recent profile pictures, eliminating the need to see each other. But, the polished stillness of these pictures belied the truth—what was captured in a smiling, innocent face poorly indicated how a person behaved face to face. Instagram deepened this divide.

Skype—which Microsoft acquired for $8.5 billion— pulled me closer to family and friends, especially after I'd moved to the U.S.

Google acquired YouTube for $1.65 billion, ensuring I was addicted to a tsunami of random videos.

I was on Twitter too, but I needed to figure out how my tweets could shine since everyone was tweeting.

LinkedIn tempted me, but who cared about professional networking? If the quest for freedom from arrested development was A, professional networking with people with zero E.Q.s might be Z — an unnecessary stretch.

Facebook changed everything, and after it bought WhatsApp for $19 billion in 2014, we knew that the influence of social media wouldn't disappear any sooner.

I was a school WhatsApp group member in the 2010s for two years. The person who created it remained the admin long before he—upon consensus or otherwise—democratized it by making every 50+ members a group administrator. Most members were in India, and the rest were from across the globe.

Two people—including the one who created the group—who were best friends had a financial tiff. One had allegedly owed the other close to half a million Indian rupees.

When their coffee didn't brew in person, the lender brought up the matter of his roasted ground beans in the group chat. He tried brewing it by naming and shaming the borrower and his family, not realizing that profanity wouldn't separate liquid coffee from the used grounds. The borrower, not offering a convincing explanation in his defense to the group, still needed to roast his coffee beans.

The best friends kicked each other out of the group. They could repeat this feat because they were instantly added upon deletion by a few friendly group members since everyone was a group admin. Hurt not only by the naming and shaming but by being deleted, the creator of the group, the borrower, removed everyone from the group before adding them, minus the lender, and becoming the sole group admin, like before.

The best friends' trust in each other had died alongside the death of compassion. The e-intimidation, instead of a heart-to-heart talk, became an accepted civilness. Nobody was shocked. We were waiting for this.

If the hunt for freedom stocked up its shares on a single Microsoft window in the mid-90s, the 2020s has opened many applications without offering a wholesome view. These apps continue to close our eyes to any possibility of viewing, witnessing, or experiencing the real. A WhatsApp forward or Facebook post could get someone killed.

Before it's too late, everyone must realize that our life can't be end-to-end encrypted in the evil deceit of applications.

***

## Accent is Ak-sent

Two decades ago, while working in Delhi, I met Indians who'd traveled from the U.S. for month-long vacations in

India. I'd known them before they'd moved to the U.S.
for employment. What struck me about their conduct
after five years in the U.S. was how they'd developed an
accent and would converse only in English.

In the mid to late nineties, such a dramatic change in a
person returning from a foreign country reeked of a
pretense, polished in arrogance. What needed to be
polished, though, was their accent.

But I was wrong to have judged them.

My wife and I moved to the U.S. ten years later. In the
first year of our life in New Jersey and New York, I was
determined not to imitate an American and ridicule my
culture by speaking like a New Yorker—although
America gave us our bread and butter. And since how I
pronounced my words mattered, I asked an American in
New York City, "Where is Path Station?" pronouncing
Path like our Indian/British 'footpath.'

"What?" he shouted. The disdain in his eyes. Since a
white man insulted a brown man, I stood my ground by
stressing how we pronounced Path like 'swath' in India.
"The train station is here," he sneered.
I should have sounded Path like his 'wrath.' I vowed to
learn the accent for words I used daily so that local
speakers understood me.

I learned how by using syllable stress correctly—the
word address could be pronounced differently. President
Obama's inaugural *uh-dres* mentioned his new *ad-res*.

The journey to improve the accent had several embarrassing stops. But I understood that I should do as Americans do in America.

Months later, I phoned a *plume(r)*, not plum-ber, to discuss an issue in the kitchen sink. After he *kwo-ted* a price I was happy with, he asked me when we could *skedj-ul* his visit.
"Wed-nes-day, 10 AM," I said.
"*Wenz-day*? Sounds fine."

He arrived as planned — six-and-a-half feet tall, heavily built Caucasian who perhaps doubled as a Santa Claus during Christmas. Impressed, I asked him what his mode of transport was.
"I came in my *vee-e-kl*," he said.
"Vee-e-kl? Vehi-cle."
He grinned before bending down to check the sink drain and pivot rod. "Two *wi-min* changed lanes, and their car bumped mine. They didn't bother to stop."
"Did you call po-leece?"
"Couldn't call *puh-leece*."
"Could you note down the plate number?"
"Yes," he said.
A minute later, he stood up and advised that I buy a new shut-off valve since the current one wouldn't last long. I paid him his fee before fulfilling my Indian courtesy.
"Des-ert in a ba-ool."
"*Dizz-urt* in a *bo-hl*? Sounds delicious. Next time." He left.
Time flew by.
We spoke as much Hindi (national language) and Malayalam (regional language) at home, saving

Indianized British English with an American accent for work and social gatherings.

Speaking British English was like eating a vegetarian thali on a full stomach. We had to consume spicy curry bowls of vernacular, slang, and jargon specific to Indian languages since we'd thought in those languages before gobbling down the kheer (pudding) of British English. The aftermath was nauseating but tolerable since this way of life had become a staple, growing up among middle-class households in Indian cities. But by adding an American accent to it, we were struggling to keep our identity intact.

Now: after spending a decade in the U.S. as a resident and a parent, I was doing almost fine with my accent. I had to relearn words and how they sounded, breaking up Hinglishalayam into Hindi, English, and Malayalam. The mantra: I had to *d-vay-lup*, not dae-vay-lup, an interest to break this up, which was emotionally challenging.

Last year, my kid said during spring break, "I want to eat something special."
"Pi-za?"
"It's *peet-zha*, papa. You always forget." His perfect accent. I wondered if he'd grow up as an American-Born-Confused-Desi (desi = Indian) or if I'd aged like an Indian-Born-Confused-Indian in America.

I am as bewildered as the people I wrongly judged twenty years ago. They weren't snobs but were trying to perfect their accents and language. And it wasn't a show-off but rather an unending work in progress, triggered by their subconscious to sound better than before.

But I'm confident that whenever I travel to India and see my friends and family, I'd force myself to sound as desi as possible. If I don't force myself, my subliminal sidekick might take over and sound fake, exposing me to unfavorable grim-ace, not *gri-mes*, and cum-ents, not *ko-ments*.

© Mahesh Nair 2023

*Far from forgotten...*

# CHAPTER FOUR
## MADE MY DAY
## BY SHERRI MATTHEWS

### Cat Healer

You don't visit a 'Kitten Room' and leave empty-handed.
Which is how we got eight-week-old Maisy. My
youngest of three sons, Liam, had grown up with cats,
but I'd promised him his own when he was old enough.
By the time he turned ten, I could no longer deny him.
Not that I didn't want another cat, but my reluctance
came from concerns for my marriage and the chance we
might have to move.

"I'm not sure we're ready," I protested on the drive to the
cat shelter. I didn't tell my son my real excuses. And
anyway, it was futile: we both knew I'd melt as soon as

we got there.

"Don't worry, Mom," he said when we got Maisy, "I'll take care of her."

I merely nodded the way all mothers do when they hear that line. And yet... a part of me didn't doubt it. Liam had formed an especially close bond with our cat, Willow. When the pressure of school and friends got too much, he would break down in tears of frustration. I would send him to his room to cool down, not for punishment, but for the sanctuary I knew he craved. "Oh, Willow, Oh, Willow," he'd wail, scooping her up in his arms, plopping her down on his bed and sobbing salty tears on her tummy. And she let him, happily so. He would emerge a child transformed. He wouldn't be diagnosed with Asperger's Syndrome until he was eighteen, and I knew nothing about 'therapy cats'. But I knew everything about the way Willow soothed him with her unconditional love and acceptance.

I got divorced and left America for England with my children. Willow and Maisy came too. I remarried and we got our boy cat, Eddie. Sadly, we lost Willow at fourteen, but Maisy stuck to Liam like a burr through the depression and anxiety that would leave him housebound.

For fifteen years she stayed by his side, and her loss devastated him. "I can't ever get another cat," he said, "I can't go through this again." Eddie, brave and noble, took up Maisy's mantle. He would answer the call as Liam's companion, giver of trust, enduring friend.

I cuddled Eddie and prayed, please live forever.

"I've found the perfect kitten," Liam announced two years later. "She's special, I know it." My jaw dropped to the ground. He still grieved for Maisy, but what miracle was this with the passage of time? He pinged her photo across to my phone. Tiny and cute and as sweet as all kittens, but why her? Why now?

"I know she's right for us, Mom, I just know, and Eddie needs a new friend."

But I knew this wasn't about Eddie. This was about Liam willing to risk his love once more. On a little black kitten with sleek, glossy fur, claws sharp as pins and eyes that gleamed like gold. She had us at "meow".

Olive, Liam named her. Our Little Black Olive.
We were smitten and all went well. Until her spay operation. Until she stopped eating.

Late afternoon and the skies already darkening, my husband drove us to an emergency vet an hour away. Liam cradled Olive in a blanket in the front with the heater full blast. I sat in the back and wrung my hands and watched snowdrifts on the roadside zoom by my window.

The vet poked and prodded her, prescribed more pain medication and antibiotics. "If she isn't eating by morning," she said, "bring her back. It could be serious." We tried kitten milk, a morsel of chicken and gravy she would normally have wolfed down. She sniffed once, twice, and turned away. Fear flashed in Liam's eyes which I knew reflected mine. It thrummed between us, a palpable beat of our failed attempts to help her.

I called the vet and she told me to bring her straight in. I stood by the examination table with my heart in my mouth. This time, she found an open sore the size of a golf ball in Olive's groin. I gasped when she showed me. What terrible fate had befallen my kitten all of five months old?

"A burst abscess," she said and I burst into tears. Olive must have been in agony, yet not once had she bitten or struck me when I had stroked her. Nor when I picked her up, though she had winced. An infection from her spay incision had formed the abscess, it was good it had come to the surface and burst. "We can treat her, she'll be fine." The vet's kind smile bathed me in relief.

I brought Olive home wearing a medical t-shirt to stop her from licking her wound. It fit snuggly from her neck to the base of her tail. She walked like a toy with stiff wooden legs, and her long, thick tail swished side-to-side.

Olive got her shirt and I got the 'flu. For several days in that first winter of her life, we curled up together on a chair by the fire and shivered and shook our way to recovery. The removal of her shirt two weeks later revealed a smooth, shiny patch where the sore had been. Now we could all heal. Settle down.
Then the pandemic struck.

Confined to the house during lockdown, Olive delighted in our all-day company. She discovered new antics. Like helping my husband when he worked from home with arranging his paperwork by sitting on it.

Like racing past me on the stairs dodging my crutches which I needed after breaking my ankle out walking. In the spring, she sat in the porch by the window and watched blossom from the cherry tree float past.

One day to the next grew weary. I longed to see my older sons when lockdown meant many months without a visit. I wanted to wrap them in my arms and say to their faces, I love you. Olive brought boundless energy to my malaise. She kept my smile alive.

Bringer of joy and shadow by night.

Liam found refuge all-night gaming with his online friends, Eddie at sleep by his side. Olive nested with me between my feet. When I tossed and turned in the small hours, she bobbed about like a boat in the harbour, anchored, safe. Constant.

One night of many of broken sleep, I sat up and reached for her, a hazy crescent shape balled up between my calves. I ran my hand along her warm, silken body and gently tickled her chin. She nuzzled my hand and buzzed my fingers with her purr. I kissed her head. It smelled of toast. I marvelled at her comfort in the dark.

I marvelled at the best therapy going in a little black cat called Olive.

\*\*\*

## Six Degrees of Separation & Thank You, Todd Fisher

I met Clint Eastwood in the summer of '81 while horse-riding in the Hollywood Hills. He was coming towards me, languidly rocking back-and-forth on his saddle, tipping his hat and said, "Howdy, Miss," as he passed by me on the narrow, dusty path. I was twenty-one and with a friend who did his best to try to convince me it wasn't him at all but a look-alike.

Though unimaginable at the time, that friend would become my husband and father to my three children. He told them what he'd told me: it wasn't him. And when I regaled them with my story, I joined in with their teasing peals of laughter: "Yeah right, Mom, sure that was Clint Eastwood!"

But had I gawped, open-mouthed like an idiot for nothing as the hero of my all-time favourite movie *The Good, The Bad and the Ugly* sauntered by? Had to be Clint, right? It's my story and I'm sticking to it.

Today the kids are more apt to say, "That's really cool."

And when I look back decades later to that encounter, I think of a certain fascinating theory known as 'six degrees of separation':

> **'Six degrees of separation** *is the theory that everyone and everything is six or fewer steps away, by way of*

*introduction, from any other person in the world, so that a chain of "a friend of a friend of a friend "statements can be made to connect any two people in a maximum of six steps." It was originally set out by Frigyes Karinthy and popularized by a play written by John Guare.'* (Wikipedia).

Because although meeting Clint Eastwood was no more than that, there are other celebrities who have encircled my life in surprising ways.

The first time I recall was on a Saturday in 1976 with my Dad at a pub somewhere in Hampshire when I was sixteen. As he held court with his fellow revellers, I got cornered in a one-sided conversation with an eccentric though harmless, grey-haired, well-spoken man. He wore yellow-checked trousers and a loud cravat and 'Shakespeare' came up once or twice. I feigned interest, secretly wishing Dad would drink up so we could leave.

Later, when I asked him about the strange, 'old' man, I was not expecting his blithe reply: "Oh, that's Freddie Jones," adding to my blank stare, "the famous actor." Famous to some but not to me. Why couldn't it have been someone like Steve McQueen? Far-fetched, perhaps, but not after hearing the rumours that one or two famous musicians frequented that same pub. Mick Fleetwood was one, at the height of his fame.

And no pun intended, but this rumour had to be true, because bizarrely – and I don't want to know how, though I can hazard a million guesses – my dad had acquired Mick's jacket. A plaid, lined lumberjack-style thing he had left behind at the pub after a drinking session. My brother ended up with it having 'borrowed it'. And when I was eighteen, I wore it on a cold night in November sat around a bonfire drinking beer with my American boyfriend at home in Suffolk.

I wonder if Mick ever thought about that jacket and what had happened to it? My darling Dad, gone but far from forgotten, would not have given that jacket a second thought. Yet he skirted on the edge of a shadowy celebrity life-style, dropping in stories about meeting Elizabeth Taylor in a bar, chatting to his boxing hero, Sugar Ray Robinson, in 1952 in New York. And snogging Joan Collins at a party in London in the sixties.

As for Freddie Jones, Dad knew him from playing Alex DeLarge's probation officer in *A Clockwork Orange*. That movie meant nothing to me then. My children were adults by the time I eventually watched it. And chatting one day with my middle boy about it and my tenuous connection with Freddie Jones, he told me this: he had a work colleague and friend in Brighton whose brother was Toby Jones, a well-known British actor. He made the connection first about their famous father.

Later, he told his friend, "My mum met your dad in a pub when she was sixteen."

But there is one celebrity six-degree moment that had a profound influence on my family life. In 2001, during my eldest son's senior year of high school in California, our then home, he was in the throes of wrapping up a movie production for its final grading. Many times he stayed late after school to finish editing on archaic equipment, causing endless frustration.

A friend of his, a girl and fellow classmate he'd known for years, offered for him and his friend to come to her home. She was sure her stepdad could help. He knew a little bit about sound production.

One evening as arranged, I drove my son and his friend to the girl's house. It was out in the middle of nowhere and I dropped them off at the top of a long drive, the house partially hidden behind a forest of trees. The story that tumbled out of him when I picked them up hours later was nothing short of incredible.

The girl, it turned out, was Vanessa Rivers. My son had no reason for it to occur to him that she was the daughter of a certain American rock-n-roll singer, Johnny Rivers. Think *Secret Agent Man*. But since her parents had split up, she now lived with her mother and her stepdad – Todd Fisher. Son of Debbie Reynolds and Eddie Fisher (who had left her for Elizabeth Taylor). And brother of Carrie Fisher – the one and only, Princess Leia.

And 'knowing a bit about sound production' was much more than an understatement. Todd Fisher had his own recording studio in his house. Oh to have been there to witness my son's face when he entered the room. In all the time he had known Vanessa, she had never given the slightest inkling of her Hollywood connections.

As they got down to business with the helpful and pleasant Mr. Fisher, my son and his friend tried to pretend that everything was normal. This proved almost impossible when the phone rang. It was Princess Leia.

Both huge *Star Wars* fans, the boys couldn't believe it. The next call came from his mother, Debbie Reynolds. Whatever it was that was said in that conversation, it seems that she gave her son a bit of a ticking off. In my son's words, he hung up and turned to him and his friend and said, "Boys, if there's one piece of advice I can give you it's this: – and it's got nothing to do with sound production – when you leave home, wherever you go, always, always, make sure to remember to call your mother."

My eighteen year old boy-man was about to launch out into the world. My nest would be emptier, one by one, until each one of my chicks flew away. I couldn't bear to think about it. But I needn't have worried, because he took these words to heart. His movie gained him a grade A, but more importantly he remembers to call me.

So, Todd Fisher, wherever you are, I want to thank you from my mother's heart. And as for Clint Eastwood, I know it was him. For the impressionable young English girl I was back then, knowing already the pain of loss, I will never forget his smile and saying "Howdy" out there on those Hollywood Hills.

Clint, Baby – you made my day.

© Sherri Matthews 2023

*No place I'd rather be...*

# CHAPTER FIVE
## BENEATH
## BY TRENT MCDONDALD

The story of this story is one of expanding an idea, and perhaps digging even farther beneath that original idea, to come up with a more fully developed narrative. A very short, preliminary version of "Beneath" was written to a prompt. I was given a photo of a small lake. There was a shallow reflection on the surface, but you could tell the water was deep. The word "beneath" was also part of the prompt.

With the photo and the key word, my first thought was of one person only being able to see the surface of another person. With the photo "in hand" (ok, on the computer), I knew I had to have the shock of a literal breaking the surface of the water for the first person to break that figurative surface to see the depth of what lay beneath.

Aren't we all like that sometimes? We only read the surface of a person without really knowing them unless there is a crisis.

When expanding this story from its original "short-short" form, besides just sketching the characters with finer details, I decided to add layers, to show that there was much more beneath the characters, such as history and family.

I hope you all enjoy!

## Beneath

The buds on the trees were about ready to burst forth in a sure sign of the arriving Spring, but Katrina didn't notice. March meant "Spring" where she came from, and she despised the fact that, with April less than a week away, it was still winter up where Uncle lived.

Almost as much as she despised Uncle. Who was he to tell her what to do? Like demanding she wear a jacket when she went outside. OK, she was shivering a little since she purposefully disobeyed him, but did he have to tell her as if she was a two-year-old? She was seven! She knew how to take care of herself. What did Uncle Charles know?

That decided it, she changed course and took the path towards the pond. Not only did Uncle tell her to never go there alone, that it was dangerous, but he stayed away from the pond himself, so it was the only place she knew she could be completely alone.

Nana had also told her the pond was dangerous, much deeper than it appeared, and the water had only thawed a couple of weeks back, but Nana had left a few days ago.

And that was the other thing, why did Nana have to leave her all by herself with Uncle? She didn't want to be there in the first place, but at least having Grandma Perkins around helped a little. And now she wasn't there.

Katrina had originally headed into the woods. If she had known where she was going, she could have taken the road as it was quicker. In fact, the old rickety dock was less than a two-minute walk from Uncle's house. But she did like the silence of the woods and it had been a nice walk amongst the barren trees, totally out of sight of any houses or humans. There were no demands on her out there. She could live in her head.

Nana and Uncle had whispered about Mom and Dad when they thought Katrina couldn't hear. She didn't get it all, but knew it was serious. Nana had told her that she had to live with Uncle for a while. Hopefully it wouldn't be long, but the days had already turned into weeks, and Nana had only been there for a couple of days at the beginning before leaving Katrina alone with Uncle. She came back a week later, making Katrina think she could finally go home, but no, Nana was just coming back to check on her.

She brought a couple of suitcases full of Katrina's clothes. Those suitcases were like a lead weight on Katrina's heart.

And then last Tuesday Nana left again.

"Don't go too close to the water!"

Uncle's voice rang in her mind as she approached the pond. She stepped out onto a rock, just to spite him. The water was smooth and clear.

She lost her balance and tottered a little, so jumped back to shore.

She didn't think she would have fallen, but if she had, Uncle would have been furious when she came home sopping wet. Would he spank her?
Uncle hated her, but never touched her. He just talked mean, mostly using "time" sentences. "Time to get up." "Time for lunch." "Time to brush your teeth and get ready for bed." "Time to turn the TV off." "Time to study." "Time to get ready to go." Time for this, that and everything.

When it wasn't "time for," he was giving her commands. "Wear your jacket, it's cold outside." "Stay away from the pond." "Sit in the backseat when we are driving." "Rinse your plate off and put it in the dishwasher."

Katrina followed the path around the pond towards the village.

One thing was for sure, Uncle hated kids and especially little girls.

There was a photo of a woman and a girl about Katrina's age on the mantle above the fireplace. Katrina discovered right away to never mention the photo or the people in it when Uncle was around, but Nana told her that it was another Katrina, her cousin. She seemed sad. When Katrina wondered aloud about there being two Katrinas, Nana told her that there were actually three. Three?

The first Katrina was Mom and Uncle's little sister. She was special and Mom and Uncle both named their daughters after her.

Nana didn't say anything else about her namesake, at

least not then, but Katrina knew that this was another one that was never to be talked about around Uncle.

The pond, actually more like what Katrina would call a lake, was mostly surrounded by the woods, but had a small village at one end. The village was really a section of the town where Uncle lived. Katrina thought that "village" was even more wrong than "pond" since all that was there was a store, a gas station and five houses. On the pond itself there was a tiny strip of sand that made up the public beach and landing for small boats and canoes. Well, at least in the warmer weather. Now in almost-April-but-still-winter, few people visited the lake and the bit of beach was almost always empty.

Just before the beach there was an ancient wooden pier sticking far out into the water. It was the first part of the pond reached when walking down the road from Uncle's house.

"Don't go out on that pier. It is old and decrepit and a board may break, tossing you into the water."

Katrina headed towards the pier.

Actually, now that she thought about it, Nana had talked about both of the previous Katrinas.
"Poor Charlie always blamed himself for everything, even if he didn't deserve it. Like with his wife and daughter. And his sister."

Nana had stopped talking for a moment. Was she holding back tears?

"My youngest came late in life and was just seven when your mom was 17 and Charlie was 21. Charlie was living with his father and had picked up a few of his dad's bad habits. If it was anyone's fault, it was their father's, but for some reason Charlie took the blame onto himself and for some odd reason your mother seemed to agree. That's most likely why you've only met Charlie at family events at my house. Also why he never boats or swims or anything. Not after that. And even the drinking that he picked up from his dad might have been made worse from it. Of course, his wife and daughter are why he no longer drinks. He feels guilty there, even though it happened years after she had left him."

Katrina had no idea what Nana was talking about when she said all of that in answer to Katrina's question on why Uncle never took her to the pond. Looking out into the pond on her walk and thinking of the two other Katrinas, it all made a little more sense.

Well, maybe not, but at least she knew who Nana was talking about.

The pier stuck out from the near end of the beach parking lot. There was a little pile of old, rotting snow at the edge of the lot, the remnants of what she knew must have been a small mountain created by the plow. "Stupid place with its stupid winter!"

Purposefully not even glancing towards Uncle's house, just to spite him and his still-winter-town, she stepped onto the first green and grey board of the pier and froze.

She had to admit that the pier was a little scary. It was twisted and some of the boards were obviously rotted. She had wanted to explore before but didn't dare. After the short pause, she took a few tentative steps out. It wasn't slippery, and on closer inspection although some of the boards were decrepit, most of the wood appeared solid. She took another couple of steps then stopped and looked around. It was a pretty little lake.

She curled her nose. It was *not* a "pond", no matter what Uncle and the locals called it!

Feeling more assured, she walked to the end of the pier and squatted down low, looking across to try to find the path she took to the shore from Uncle's house.

As she looked across the pond, a memory of a dream came back. Only she realized it wasn't a dream.

It was the first night she was at Uncle's house. She woke up in the middle of the night and could hear Nana and Uncle talking. The words were difficult to make out at first, but as she listened harder, she began to catch more of them.

"Well, I'm just worried something's going to happen is all."

"I know she's safe with you."

"*I'm* safe, but can I protect her if something happens? They were both seven, you know, just like her."

"Are you getting superstitious, now?"

"No, but it's too much of a coincidence."

"Your daughter was seven when Sheila took her away, not when they were in the accident. And how was that your fault?"

"She was seven when I last saw her, when I drove them away because I was drinking too much. And if I hadn't driven them away, they wouldn't have been in the accident and would be alive today. That's why."

"That is just plain stupid. And your sister wasn't your fault either. She was on the boat with your father. You almost killed yourself swimming from shore to try to rescue her. How are you to blame there?"

"I should have known Dad was drunk and not let him take her out."

"Bull. You knew your father and you know as well as I do that there was nothing that you could have done to stop him."

There was a little silence. Were they still talking, now too quiet for Katrina to hear? She strained her ears to catch more.

"I'm still not sure. She's so young and vulnerable. I'm not safe."

"We've been over it a thousand times, you are the only one. And you'll do fine. Really."

When she had heard the conversation, they were just meaningless words. Remembering it while on the pier, something about it changed.

"Oh, my!" Katrina said and jumped up.

She did not feel herself slip or trip. The first sign that things weren't right was the pain of the ice-cold water sending needles through her entire body. All of her muscles froze instantly. She took a deep breath to scream, but was under water.
The world went black.

***

"There you are honey. I have to say, you gave us all quite a scare!"

"Nana?"

She was in a bath of steaming water at Uncle's house. Nana was sitting on a stool by the bath.
"Yes, sweety, I came back earlier today, just after you left the house. Your uncle went out to find you."

"What happened?"

"He said he saw you at the end of the pier. As he

started out to get you, you jumped up and slipped off the end. He dove into the water and pulled you out. He was afraid he reached you too late, but was able to pump the water out and get you breathing. He then picked you up as if you were a kitten and jogged home with you in his arms. I met him at the door and took over. I stripped you and put you in the hot bath. You've only been here a second – I think the hot water woke you. You fell in maybe five minutes ago, heck, perhaps even as little as two. It happened so fast, yet it seems like slow motion.

I can finally breath again!"

"Uncle saved me?"

Nana nodded.

"Why? He hates me! He hates all kids!"

Nana's eyes filled with tears.

"Honey, how can you say that! He loves you more than you can know! He's felt guilty his entire life over losing girls that he loved, and was afraid of you. He opened his house and his heart for you. Why do you think he hates you?"

Katrina thought back. Why did she feel that way? "He always talks to me like he is angry."

"He was never angry, Kitten. He sounds gruff, but only because he doesn't know how to talk to you, what to say. He was so worried about you."

"He looks at me funny."

"Because you remind him of the other two Katrinas in his life. He lost both of them, and is worried about you."

"But he…" A shiver went down her spine and she felt the frigid water. "He saved me."

Nana smiled and leaned over and kissed her forehead. "Yes, he did."

Katrina thought for a moment.

"When will I see him?"

"I heard him finish his shower a second ago. He will head to the kitchen as soon as he's dry and changed. Unless you need something, I'll go down there now and put a kettle on. Here is a huge, fluffy towel and some warm, dry clothes. Take your time, but when you are ready, dry off, get dressed and come down to see us." Katrina nodded.

"OK, go on. I'll be down in a moment."

The world had changed. Katrina saw and heard everything that Uncle had said and done in a different light.

After a few minutes, she finally let the water out and got up.

***

Uncle jumped out of his chair. His hair was wet and his face flushed.

"How are you? Are you feeling OK?" He turned to Nana. "Mom, are you sure we don't need to take her to the emergency room?"

Katrina ran over and wrapped her arms around him. At first Uncle Charles seemed surprised, but then pulled her in tight. She could feel him sobbing.

"Thank you, Uncle," she said. "And this is for everything. Thank you for saving me. Thank you for taking me in. Thank you for caring for me so well. And forgive me."

"Forgive you, Kitten?"

"For not realizing it, for not saying all of this sooner."

He pulled back and looked down at her. He was

smiling, though there were still tears in his eyes.

"And thank you."

"For what?"

He just shook his head.

"For reminding him he is alive," Nana said. "Oh, thinking of being alive, your father is doing much better. Your mom is still not ready to have you return home, but will be soon. Will it be torture for you to stay here a couple more weeks? I can take you to my house if you'd rather."

Katrina smiled up at Uncle.

"There is no place I'd rather be than right here."

© Trent McDonald 2023

*It's the light that matters...*

# CHAPTER SIX
## GROUND ZERO
## BY JEFFREY D. SIMMONS

This chapter is an opportunity to share my journey and growth. I call this Ground Zero. The light of the mind as it sparks and engages the universe and this physical existence is captured in my poetry and rhymes through times of darkness and growth. The beautiful truth of this life journey of mine is that through it all, I am the light. My soul loves love and is a gift, as you will find, is tested and tried through time. In this life and the next, be Light!

What shall a man live for in this world of lies and half-truths? To be or not to be is NOT the question or answer. Ground Zero a moment of chance and change! The place where time and space give way to a new creation; a self-creation not supported by procreation! Again, what shall a man live for in this moment? This is my moment and mine alone to create the best me in freedom and in attitude. I hope you enjoy the 26 poems showing my perspective.

## 1. Ferrous

Taking the course of ying and yang
Flowing with the molecules
You can call them by name
Ferocious is not gracious
genius, perceived mischievous
It is the mindset of the genius!

## 2. Rules of Acquisition

Evermore knowing
Creatively growing
Positively sowing
Star seeds of
Celestial strains
That mortal man
Cannot comprehend
Or explain
Living multiple
Lives in one
dying and living
Metabolically
Outside, inside
A Vessel
of intricate design
Rules of Acquisition

dictate
I must use my mind
to expand
and
Contract
My world
My existence
Not driven by
Secular knowledge
or Spiritual
Interference
Of mere mortals
Who claim immortality
At the event
Called mortality
Universal recipient
Universal donor
Of knowledge
Antigens
Blood types
And genocidal
Wipes
Test tube babies
Stem cells
And
Clones
Rules of acquisition
Declare life is
Reflective
Connective
Collective
It's not in the
Shell

It's in the bone
Of my bone
Marrow
Flesh of my flesh
Soul of my soul
Absent of a
Duality

## 3. Levels

We are not on the same level
I do eat greens, beans, and chicken
Wings
We not on the same level
You scared of your God
And blame the devil
When your life falls apart?
We not on the same level
You hoard stuff and things
Chase money
And ATM machines
We are not on the same level
It's not that I am better than you
Or even open my mouth
To judge or be judged
It's the boundaries I set in place
To keep myself, my soul in peace
And safe
Oh it's me being me
Living more than a best life
Living this life is not at all
My best
Unless your life is the test

Of how your past lives
Were or were not your best
Continuity of being
Who and what I Am
Naw sisters and brothers
I am not your nigga
If I don't get no bigger
See we aren't on the same level
Bill Cosby took a fall
The say behind a pill
A 60-second thrill
Well I don't know Bill
but he was way above
My level
So you better be clear
About the devils you create
Only self has to eat from
That plate
I don't hate
Neither do I perceive
That stuff, sex, and thangs
Will fill the void
Of self-worth
Where my soul
Is bold
And shines through
The pains of this life
This dimension of comedy
Scenes and attractions
Distractions
Factions
Actions that are Willy Nilly
Touchy feely

Abrupt and silly
We not on the same level
But you are welcome
To sit at my table
Because I am able
To eat alone
So if you bring
Attitude
And
Negativity
Miss me with that
For I am on a different level
Defying gravity
Illusions and delusions
I am the constant
process of Soulful evolution
We are not on the same level
Do you, Be You
That's my personal solution

## 4. Addiction

I looked at the affliction
Called addiction
It can be found
In every fabric of life
Its constant friction
Applied to the substance
of the unknown
The illiteracy of self
Mental obsessions
And Spiritual health
I looked at the reflection

Did a five-point inspection
Of my ego inflated 'Eid
Obvious that to grow
You have to know
What fertile soil is
Fertilizer
Naturalizer
Neutralizer
The imperative
declarative
That to thine own self
Be true
You alone are accountable
For the things you allow
And the things that you do
Pretty it ain't
I am not a saint
But I am in this fight
I won't faint
I have a future to manifest
A landscape to paint
With opportunities grandeur
Details of perfection
Made by mental selections
Of my genuine affections
Clarified by actions
Changing frequencies
Channels and songs
That the level of my
Success
Is indirectly related
To my external and internal
Mess

So I confess
That with all my
Soul and might
I am winning
This spiritual
And
Physical fight!
I can
For
I Am!

## 5. Get It

Where's the fun sitting on the log
Watching and waiting for the stand too fog
Phases of the season don't need a reason
To respond with adept treason
In a sphere held by the gravity of fear
Get it
It's waffles and chicken
Catfish and grits
Ice cream and cake
Coochie and cock
That maintains the status quo
Of the ring in tub
Or Orion in the sky
And shadows in the closet
Waiting for the battle cry
To vacate
And women to lactate
Wait
Super imposed
Like nobody knows

The inner-standing of hate
Got a lot of side dishes on my plate
Hate can wait
Truth can placate
Lies can fly
I don't have time to cry
Empires are falling
And rising to the occasion
Some would call my Bronze people
Simply amazing
Yet I know and understand
That we are phasing
Into
Seasons
Reasons
Frequencies
And vibrations
That is becoming increasingly
The Bronze nation
Feel the sensation of the best
Of the drums
Sounds like that old beat
Our ancestors used to him
Red rum red rum red rum
Out with the old
And in with the new
Evolution
Solutions
Conclusions
This ain't about no God or devil
Get it
Are you ready for the next level?
Either you are or you not

Royalty and sovereignty
Marks the Spot
Connect the dots
Drop knowledge like it's hot
Into the minds and souls
Of the children
Our legacy
Build up
And tear down
False kingdoms
And fools who have crowns
Strengthen our children
Feed our children
Own our ground
And Stand
Bronze Woman and Man
Cause we Can
And have
Get it

## 6. Confession

It was an obsession
Then my eye's dried
And were clear
It wasn't love
It wasn't last
It was an apparition
Of my own mind
So I was inclined to seduce
Self with material wealth
Forsaking my mental and spiritual
Health

My obsession became malignant
And that's when I became cognizant
That it's my mind and mine alone
That can heal itself within itself
That is true wealth
Not obsession or possession
But self-reflection and self-confession
I call it progression

The Words the Word

Pronunciation
Insinuation
Exclamation
Offer
Proclamation
Of the Word that comes
From my mouth
As I speak it
I create it
My divinity
Bought forth
In trinity
Slow to speak
Quick to hear
Mind, body, Soul
The trinity of the words
I create
gestated upon
the fabric of time
My words are a reflection of
my mind
Drawn from the heart

Unstable at times
If I speak it
Fluently
Congruently
It's true
Cause I decided
To let those words through
So by words amiss
You can NOT define me
No words you conjugate
Define me
Two words that still
Perform
My will
I am that
I am
Consequently, whatever I say
Lights my way
And creates my day!

## 7. What Jeffrey Forgot

Reciprocity of a Singularity
A platitude of knowing
Who and what you are
Twinkle bright
Morning Star
Suns of the mourning
When divinity
Was explained as a trinity
When all within
Was demonized and called sin
Familiar cords that bind

Life and blood
Umbilical
Equivocal
Biblical principles
And commands
Issued by a two legged man
For who knows how long
Jeffrey's head had been
Buried in the sand
There's a whole lot of dirt
My people hurt
Theirs is no rhyme or reason
To stay in this season
And commit treason to my
Soul
Waiting FOR the TRUTH
To be told
Why should I wait
For hate
To be my dinner plate
Fate it cannot be
Cause I create my reality
By thought
By word
My soul revelates
Mysteries yet told

## 8. Closed Doors

It ain't about why
Ain't no story worthwhile
To be told or sold
Closed doors is

The doors
That are open
Predestined to
Produce
Construct
And define the
Element of the mind
The season of
Truth
That closed doors
Are forever
Open
To
You
The real true you
On your level
Not God or a devil
But the closed doors
That took you up
To the next vibration
Creation
Closed to most
Open to you
True

## 9. That Strength

The power went out
For three days in a row
They said it was an ice storm
That's a lie
What's the truth?
It's a black out

Designed to test you
Busy here busy there
Genocide is real
Self-imposed
People
Be vigilant and wise
The Black out
Is the disguise
Of bar codes and GMO's
Chem-trails
And jail cells
FEMA coffins
And camps
For roaches and ants
No fire wood in the hood
No lights to see
Use the spirit and soul
Change the frequency
Keep drinking
Drugging
And thugging
Time would be better
Spent
Unplugging
Hugging
Staples and pillars of truth
Left by the ancestors
That kept them free
That strength
That lives
In
You and me

## 10. Victory

Manufactured summations
Of institutionalization
Propagation
Education
Integration
Segregation
Still on the plantation
Cause we don't own the land
No-one can
Nubile and strong
This earthly tomb
Is not our home
Planted here for a season
Reason
Clandestine destinations
We are more than a nation
We are the protons
Neutrons
Electrons
Creation
Spanning time unknown
Planted here in this realm
Until we mature
And have grown
Understand that it's not
Success we chase
Or War we wage
Our Victory is timeless
Hold up don't turn the page
Here the wisdom of
the Oracle

the Sage
The mystery of the victory
Is not found on a page
The power is in our soul
Restated and gestated
Hated by all
Because we stardust of
A rare kind
We exist and persist
Throughout the ages
Of time
Our Victory is Sweeter
Than a thousand-year aged
Wine
Because we are the
Manifestations of darkness
Divine
We have souls
That are the lights of time
Say la Victory
Rewind

## 11. I Write

I write because I see
I write because I am free
I write because I'm happy
I write because I am me
Twisted by lies
Tales woven by
The Lord of Flies
Chicanery of sorts
I retort

Bogus allegories
Scripted programs
None of the above
Can describe who I Am
I watched my mother
With child beat mercilessly
By the man supposedly
The husband
I heard her cries
The brutality went deep
Into my soul it did creep
The pain of his fists
Hitting me too
What is a child supposed
To do
I wrote then to escape
The wrath of disdain
Found myself grown-up
Trying to numb the pain
Thrust into life without a clue
Why do people do
The things that they do
Could utopia exist?
Paradise
A sanctuary of peace
Yes, I discovered it
Exists in the fabric
Of my mind
That's truthfully where
I do my time
I exonerated the pain
Shame, false pride and guilt
Looked inside myself

And embraced the miracle
The universe has built
So I write not by fright
Or flight
I write because
Once I was blind
But now My soul
Has sight and
Strength to fight
For my truth
And my truth alone
I no longer
Am a chess piece
A rook or a pawn
I am immortal
Prince of the Universe
King of my moment
Master of none
I write because
There can be only one
Me!

## 12. Beats

May I have a beat
Huh
Tap your feet
Snap your fingers
Hear this track
A sway back
Where two hearts beat
As one
Standing on the banks

Of the Nile
A band of my ancestors
Coming for me
Adorned in purple robes
Celestial pearls
Who overcame the secular
Trappings of this world
By ascension
And assassination
Of the lower guides
That act as a veil
That covers the soul
Which is your eyes
Now let's move to the
Ears your sense of sound
Feel the symmetry
Feel the beats
And the rhythm
Of multiple heartbeat
Making music in harmony
In the conscious of
The soul
You now understand
Your journey is not
To be sold
Or told
You are the myelinated
Royalty brazen
And assured
That it's the darkness you
Are wrapped in
That they fear
But you adore

For your light in
Only shines in the darkness
You are the Gods of
Creation
Procreation
Through
Times and Ages
For ever more
Wake up!

## 13. Lights So Shine

Do you understand
I suppose the juices
Of your vibration
Libation
Every sensation of your
Being
Is in my nostrils
My cells
Traveling at light speed
To my heart and soul
I drink of your vessel
And all is well within my soul
I become bold
Then bolder
Here is my shoulder
My back is your estate
I was created to carry
You
A specified weight
For your plate is divine
From your head to

Your pretty toes
From your character within
And that casual grin
Your energy
Combines with minds
And Equalizer it is
The marinade
Started with a word
Tossed back and forth
Birthing poetic prose
And your therapeutic
Voice
Left me
Us no choice
But to turn out the
Lights
And let our
Lights so shine
Cause and effect
It's our moment
In time
To create our world
Solely by using our
Minds
And
Combines
Soul power
To together we ascend
We shine
Not because of our grind
It's just
Our time!

## 14. Why Not?

Laying on a borrowed couch
Going on three months
In a row
Not because I'm a slouch
But because I had no
Where else to go
Revealed some lessons
And truths from
The past
It's better to be on
Your own
Than kiss anybody's
Ass!

## 15. Hood King

Talking about a hood King
Holding his head up
Chin tucked in
Back straight
Cause in the hood
It is and it ain't all good
Just the thought
I wish a mofo would
Try and steal our hope
Behind the currency of
Dope
Nope
I am a Hood King
Know nothing better
Than feeding myself

My people
By any means necessary
I wear my crown
I get down
And will lay you down
Don't let the smooth taste
Fool you
I am here to school you
Life is a many splendid
Things
You gotta have a Queen
To know what I mean
Boss up
Or sit down
Gunplay ain't for the feeble
Or wannabe clowns
It's all about the stable
And my personal banker
Chemistry
Mystery
Afghan Peru
I am A Hood King
My truth is
Not to be glorified at all
It's to be my brothers and sisters
Keeper
Because we all do fall!

## 16. To Postulate

There is an institution
For the infrastructure
Called life

It's the constitution
Of self-evolution
An inventory of one's
Mind
The critical two
Freedom and time
Well what's the honor
Of wealth
Without mental health
The synopsis of
Spiritual discipline
Freedom and time
To postulate!

## 17. Your Heart

The days of time no longer
Change
They hold the same shade
And color of the ages
Yet the love that is in me
Has been flamed
It's been renewed
For such a time as this
When the love is waxed cold
That my Father's children can
Stand and be bold
In the power of his love
Tried and true
That it will take more than money
To take you through
Inspiration
Aspiration

Revelation
Not most
But some
Are willing to care
Yet out of the mouth
Of a child
Who you are is made plain
You are a good person
The world is changed
But you refused
Your heart is the same

## 18. Opposite Inflection

Sitting in the fabric of what
You see
Does not change
Because of anything
You do
You are bound
Or set free
Places to eat
Tis not
Hot
Gravity of your vibration
Frequency older than this
The equivalent
Of influence
By paths unknown
Wanting to know
What is
What is not
For getting

Or giving
Nothing
But attention
Hold up don't turn
The page
Don't
Try stroking
Not your ego
Or Id
What did
The governor say
When life was given
To the evidence
Of estate
Bold
You
Are to walk this way
Regardless of the time
Given
Everything pays
To someone
Or something
A connection
Not known
Just being told
So you understand
How
Even though I don't have
What is evident
You got a hope
That is what you are
Hitting paths
And trails

Sliding back and forth
Between water, fire, and wind
Fortunately, it's not your design
It's wait for you to truly
Know what you are hearing
See riding alone
You are but
A rare kind
And must go through
The veil
Of the womb
To be a reality
Not
False but true
Look
At the opposite of the inflection
Look at your mane
Not the cash
Make believe shit
Not depressed or stress
Where is here
This internal mess
Not a test
Wearing the mantle of
Incarceration
Incarnation
Freestyling
On what's between
Your ears
Dam each moment
Can and will change
Not shocking
When you blind

And it is not
A defect
It's the
Getting up in the grave
Which don't exist
Because you are a creation
Of mist
And paradise
Not nice
Or mean
Good or evil
Not in between
Just a being unseen
Self

## 19. Cadillac Tricking

By all means necessary or not
I'm rolling that Caddy
Off your lot
I'm profiling and styling
In the hood
Proclaiming victory
Cause I'm driving a Cadillac
With eight pistons
Under the hood
Placking two axels
And slanging that wood
Lying on the phallus
In order to get Alice
Fronting that I live
In a Palace
Drinking from a chalice

Of malice
Capricious chicanery
Cadillac tricking
Living a lie of posterity
Which is a false hood
Of reality
I sleep by the furnace
In my mom's
Basement
It's time to come clean
Cadillac tricking
Is a loss
Faking to be a Boss
Cost
More than 4 wheels
The price paid
To elevate and win
Requires wisdom
Of self
Not material
Or
Nor rims of Gold
It requires strength
Of Character
To stand alone
But not alone
To be bold
Tricking ain't tricking
When you
The brick
And you pass the
First and last lick
Cripping and pimping

Is a lame game when
The Cadillac
You driving
Not even in your name
Criss Cross
Upside down
If you Cadillac tricking
Your brand
Is that of a clown
What matters most
Is who is driving
Arrogance or Pride
Now Are you sure
You still want to
Ride

## 20. Levity

The watchers watch
The children play
The workers work
The seasons change
Levity
The scale is not zeroed
So the weight is arbitrary
Levity
Balance is not the goal
Simplicity is to be whole
From spirit to Soul
Traps, nets and webs
Are set for those who
Are Soul
Levity

Is the brevity
Of the breaths
From young to old
So how much money
Guarantees your crown
Will be pure gold
Not fool's gold
And you have no Soul
Levity is the Soul
Love never gets old

## 21. Proclivity

Facts or habits
Proclivity
The tendency to choose
To do something regularly
To live by labels
To exist in a box
To be a widget
Of industrialization
And globalization
Proclivity
To be or not be
Free
Stretching the mind
Beyond the sublime
Reconstituting time
Without hitting
Rewind
Proclivity
Is the evidence of
Predictability

Yet
I don't live by labels
Neither do I live in a box
These words I drop
They are hot
Purposefully spoken
Meant to hit that spot
The cavity of the brain that
Mirrors the soul
That part of you that's
Ageless
It never grows old
I am that man
With purpose
Of self
And mind
I am here because
My soul chose
To step out of
The illusion
Called time
And explain
Proclivit-able
Results
Of doing the same things
Out of habit
Repeating histories of
Someone else's mind
Eating unhealthy food
Off your enemies
Tables and plates
I am not here
To preach or teach

Hate of self
Or others
I am here to
Demand respect and reverence
For our mothers
The daughters and creators
Of life itself
The true resource
Of value in this
Realm called earth
Is the vessel known
As woman
To she who gives birth
Man you are an anomaly
That doesn't have to exist
Yet you persist
In the mist
Of gestational
Fortitude of progeny
Mother earth
Her reflection is the
Womb Man
And her powers
Are greater than any man
Or more valuable
Than any land
Do you know your
Position
You odious
Contemptible creature
Called man
Out of habit you create to destroy
But hear this life

Is not a toy
A woman is always a woman
But you will always
Remain a little boy
When you treat the woman like
A toy
There is no treaty
There is no compromise
There is no diplomacy
No return to sender
No outside force
Or equatorial lenders
That doesn't know
Oh man that you were created to
Defend her
Not to offend her
Nor be a pretender
Spin this edition
Editorial of good will
Like the tablets and books
That you pass along
As facts
And summations
Of what's lawful
And what's real
Be it said as I decree
You will evolve no further
Until your mind
Is set free
And you respect me
Beyond habits
Tribalism
What you call humanity

Is actually
What it is
Proclivity
A habitual tendency
Which is also slavery
Free your mind
And see the rainbow of your soul
It's more valuable than a lot of
Gold
Or the Greatest lie ever
Told!

## 22. All I See

I was once afraid
That you were a dream
I saw you as an Empress
But I didn't feel like
An Emperor
Then your softness
And prose
Was an aroma
Of hope
On the sunrise
Especially when I gazed
Into your eyes
All I see is Truth
You wear no disguise
Yea I thought to myself
And what I have been through
What I deserve
I find it all in you
Without apologizing

Or philosophy
Oh Great Oracle
Of time and Space
I know who and what
God is
When I look at your face
Imprinted in my soul
Is the fabric
Of your being
Your scent
Your walk
And your methodical
Stance
Not chance
But a multiverse
Celestial dance
So I hold the vision
Of you true
Do what you do
Do you
But I have been prepared
For this season
For you
Ado
Just keeping it real
And true

Evidence

I saw what I said
Was offensive to your
Reality
Yet I speak now

Of Actuality
That which is
And cannot be undone
By history, Google, props,
Or song's
Actuality is above the reach
Of Reality which is shaped
And spun
Trick photography
Or lip sync
Neither the dried up ink
Will make a black elephant
White or pink
Think

## 23. Right

The beginning of our relationships
Is not found on a page
But in your heart and soul
This is right
Not flesh
And the things I do
But who am I
I am
Every day is a day
To recover the right
Relationship
With the fire of your soul
Right
Will compel you
To kneel
Heal

And confess that you are not
What is right
But are being made
Into the purpose
Of. Your being

No More

Here to therefore
I ran until I could run
No more
From self-known as
Flesh and bone
The ying of my yang
The source of my eternal
Flame
Known by many names
I know it's called Soul
Which hangs on the
Latitude and longitude
Of space and time
Not fabricated
Or self-Created
Satiated
With energy
Vibrations
Frequencies
Requencies
Making the mind and soul
One power
Whole
Forever
Eternal

Yes
I ran from
The truth
I am
Is more than
Mortal man
Skipping this dimension
I wish I could
But the Sovereign Creator
Knows better
And is all that is good
Shake it up
And speak it right
Your existence
Is and will always
Be an eternal fight of flight
Of positive celestial energy
And negative terrestrial
Energy
Bona fide
Reflections
Of the Sun
Where all life
Began
To be a humble
Servant of our Father
Through trials and tribulations
Tried by fire without

## 24. A Huge Lesson

And on the 3rd day
Of this journey in time

My lesson was blatant
Fueled with fire
Made me look at self
And fallacious desires
Could have cost me my life
But it didn't
Yet I paid with a side swipe
Of the car
A flat tire
To make me sit still
And hear the universe
My ancestors speak
Their will
Silver cords of affection
That bind you
To people
Places
And things
Are not genuine
On their part
It's you who carries
The infinity spark
You seek belonging
Loving
Friendship that do
And don't exist
Stop playing games
With self
And being on ignorant
Stupid
Bullshit
Quick wit
Pro

Quo
Don't you know
Your thoughts
Is your vibe
That attracts a Vibe
Master your thoughts
Censor your mouth
Speak life
Not toxicity
Live your purpose
Be what you desire
Create your destiny
Co-op the pin
Hold up the chin
It ain't sinning
When ya winning
So celebrate the haters
Tools of progression
Remember life
In itself is
A huge lesson!

## 25. Sepsis

What I saw last night
stopping by the
Best Soul Food Shack
Sparked this fact
This concrete jungle
Breaks the Bronze
families BACK
We ain't all educated
Integrated

The poor live segregated
Subjugated
Hated by the outside
Killed from the inside
Clowned by self-pride
That they pimp, hustlers
And hoes
Generations
After generations
This story ain't new
Its malignant
Its old
The barbecue is good
The sauce got a twang
Listen to the
Mommas and daddy cry
They babies got
Broken wings
Sing star seeds
Hope is what they need
Not dope
Or governmental
Religious systems
That keep them
On their knees
Please
Don't pontificate
Fucking and making
Babies
Behind the cinder blocks
Gates
Listening to lyrics
That vilify

Self-hate
Nullification
By a piece
Of paper
A promissory note
We all regardless
Of education or class
In the same sinking boat
Gloat if you will
Our souls are 666
You can't kill
This Trojan
This virus
Is part of this
Matrix
A squeaky wheel
That it's from the bottoms
That we build
Brick by brick
Stick by stick
Stone by stone
Child by child
Woman by woman
Man by man
This is our land
United we stand
By every frequency
Vibration
And band
Cause
This ain't over
We are more than
Kings and Queens

We are more
Numerous
Than
Seashores
Or sand
We can rise
And restore
The
Light
In the
Eyes
Of our legacy
Our souls
Cause
We are eternal
Beings
We have been
Here
Before his
Story
Was told
We are the silver
And the refined
Purified
Gold
And this time
Our
Victory
Shall be bold
Let our truth
Be told!
Or sold
Not for sale

We own
Heaven and hell

## 26. Infrastructure

The evidence is subjective
This reality objective
The powers to be protective
Of a clause
Not Santa Clause
Religion or Science
What clause may that be?
Hidden in plain sight
So the blind can see
and seeing made free
The clause that is hidden
Doesn't exist
No more than planets
and history
Phantoms of a projection
From a reel to reel
The infrastructure
Of this dimension
Has always been
It would take thousands of
years to lay highways
and byways
Carve mountains
lay pipes
How about this
Technology is not new
It  is just a keynote
A keystroke

A swipe
Or better yet
A wipe
Of the mind
A program. Engineered
To validate what the unsuspecting
mind considers to be years
So where are you
Eternal being as you are
How about
You are a star
Within a Star
The truth is in you
There is no need
to look that far!

## Purpose

Yes, everything is within that I need. I looked at the man in the mirror and he looked back, I think. The question the man in the mirror asked is captured in the prose and poems of this chapter, "What is my purpose?"

After careful and selective meditation, prayer and replaying the video of my life, I have only one purpose regardless of darkness. Be Light! Be Love, Jeffrey. It's the light that matters for within its spectrum you will find shadows, prisms, portals, darkness, chaos, and creation herself. And most importantly, you will find love.

You are love Jeffrey! Be Light!
That's Ground Zero!

© Jeffrey D. Simmons 2022

*Survival to thrival...*

# CHAPTER SEVEN
## CAREGIVER BURNOUT
## BY MIKE F. MARTELLI

Over the last few years, both authors, Yvette Prior and me, Mike, have engaged in caregiving. In this chapter, the focus is on how I, Mike, have come to experience 24-hour caregiving and the first-hand challenges, burdens, exhaustion, and depletion that can lead to burnout. In addition to my caregiving experience, I have consulted and counseled people for over 35 years about caregiving.

This chapter has involved not just assessment and information provision, re: the burdens, responsibilities and stresses, but individual and group treatment and generalized promotion of adaptive coping and optimized function and self-care throughout the caregiving process. This includes recovering from burnout. As a semi-retired health and rehabilitation neuropsychologist, I am dedicated to completing a major interest, a work on a coping/rehabilitation model and methodology that was developed over a 30+ year period in practice (*Holistic Habit and Self-Rehabilitation & Growth*).

Over the last 2+ years, my wife and I have been active 24-hour caregivers, not just for her mom with dementia, but also for my sister-in-law with chronic developmental challenges. We took them into our house to provide caregiving after my mother-in-law with early dementia began having falls, one of which resulted in a significant dual impact brain injury that produced deterioration in function and requirement for 24-hr supervision. For both of these relatives, cognitive deficits are amplified by emotional challenges that have exaggerated coping deficits, especially in terms of anxiety, cognitive rigidity and a history of having been overly indulged.

Over the many previous years, a significant part of my practice has included helping to optimize coping in caregivers who too often experience significant distress, fatigue emotional exhaustion and burnout. It was in that context that I have borrowed, adapted, developed and refined an armamentarium of strategies to assist caregivers in coping.

These strategies addressed challenges faced by the parents, spouses, significant others and family members of persons with an array of neurological injuries and diseases from brain injury to stroke to dementia, in addition to neuromuscular, chronic pain, developmental and most other chronic diseases and disabilities.

I've treated a lot of parents and partners, including wives but also some husbands, as well as children from childhood through adult ages, albeit mostly daughters, of persons with strokes, brain injuries, spinal cord injuries, dementia and other neurologic and physical disorders, developmental disorders and diseases of aging, chronic pain and pretty much all of the common chronic diseases. Burnout is rampant and presents the major obstacle to effective caregiving and occurs in a matter of degrees in most persons. At least mild burnout, usually displayed in degrees of depression and anxiety, seems to occur in about 50% of caregivers.

The incidence varies in proportion to family assistance, family size and available help, as well as severity of disabilities and degree of difficulty in managing the person with the disease, along with instrumental factors like financial or family resources. In this chapter, some strategies for assisting coping and optimizing caregiver function while ultimately combating burnout will be presented via *The Caregiver Survival (to Thrival) Rules*.

It should be emphasized that these rules have continued to be adapted, modified, and informed by our direct, 24-hour caregiving experience.

*** 

## Caregiver Survival to Thrival

Caregivers cannot take care of anyone if they BURN OUT from not taking care of themselves. The signs of caregiver burnout include not eating properly, feeling unbalanced emotionally, feeling overwhelmed, starting to withdraw, interacting less with peers, having less mental focus at work, and/or difficulty maintaining usual grooming and appearance.

The best antidote for preventing and treating burnout

is early intervention. The following can assist with that goal.

## 1. Self-Care

Caregivers cannot take care of anyone if they are burned out and the first antidote involves self-care. For starters, try scheduling one half day per week off for rest and relaxation, in some form of recreation that *does not* involve helping, caregiving, treating, or being responsible for ANYONE else or their needs.

Ask for help as needed and try to build up to one full day OFF for replenishment. Then, work up to 1.5 or 2 full days, etc. If possible, try to move toward limiting caregiving to the amount of 40 hours per week.

It is in both the caregivee and caregiver's best interest to learn to easily and openly ask others for both emotional and instrumental help!

It is imperative that full time caregivers engage in relationships with relatives and friends who give support (more than they seek or need it) for problems and needs.

## 2. Support Areas to Consider:

- Emotional support (i.e., patient listening, without impatience, interjections or efforts at quick fixes, which circumvents the most powerful therapeutic healing, being understood (cf "Men are from Mars & Women are from Venus") - see appendix (p13) for elaboration.

- Instrumental (practical help that is requested) for the sake of the caregiver and caregivee.
- Ensure that in other parts of life, and in other relationships, most of the focus is on non-caretaking activities, not helping, listening to or attending to the needs of others.

## 3. Caregiver-Caregivee Interaction

**At least some of the caregiver-caregivee** interaction must include non-caretaking activities - i.e. interaction in the patient's areas of residual strengths and competencies - especially for leisure activities. ---> *RX: Perform an inventory of previously or possibly enjoyable activity and start planning and experimenting. Non-caretaking activities strengthen the relationship and augment caregiver health.*

It is in both the caregivee and caregiver's best interest to learn to easily and openly ask others for both emotional and instrumental help!

## 4. Aim to Be a Mirror and not a Sponge

Sponging is absorbing another person's negative emotions or anger and reacting to them with similar negative emotions. It is catching the other person's negative emotions and allowing them to control your emotions and reactions.

Mirroring is the process of simple, matter-of-fact reflecting back another person's negative emotions (e.g., *"You are angry that I did not come when you first called...Hmm"*). Try to do this without (a) emotional reaction, (b) obligation to respond emotionally, or (c) obligation to agree or disagree, and, importantly, (d) without "catching" the emotion & making their problem your own.

By its nature, mirroring involves a slow, deliberate and open look at the other person statements, and prevents escalation of emotions, allowing you to control your emotions by not reacting. It allows under-reacting and keeping a cool head to help calm the situation. Besides not letting another person's problem become your own, it can help to defuse their emotions so that they can better hear their message with calmer emotions and more objectivity.

Understand that resentment of caregivers by caregivees is a too often inevitable emotional reflex because the necessity of receiving help often forces painfully devastating confrontation with deficits, disability & losses in independence and autonomy (by which most persons define themselves) - it forces the confrontation with and reminds of the awfully unwanted need for help. This is especially true for persons accustomed to being in charge and being the caregiver and not the caregivee. Understanding, practice of under-reacting, and ventilation can help.

Contract with each other to allow mistakes & not beat each other up when mistakes are made or problems occur. Learn and take into account what to monitor and remember while moving through a crisis.

## Rules of Crisis

- During crisis, everyone will be at their worst!
- Behavior and communication will reflect our/their worst!
- We/they will hold others more accountable and then excuse ourselves/ themselves!
- When we are hurting, we fail to appreciate their hurt!
- Things will get better or worse after a crisis, but will not stay the same!

## Counter Measures

- Blame the situation only.
- Avoid and work toward NOT blaming each other
- Try to understand each other's feelings and stresses
- Bolster each other working together
- Work as a team and have the common goal of reducing stress.
- Learn, remember, and apply these counter measures

## Personal Example

For me, caregiving represented a significant interruption of my intended retirement plans. First COVID-19 prevented desired travel and overseas volunteer work, but that was relatively minor compared to related life stress that negatively impacted my marriage. For the caregiving stresses, I was able to maintain a good sense of humor and some hobbies and exercise that were pretty effective. For family stresses that were solvable but instead enabled, I lost my reliable sense of humor while the hobbies and exercise were less effective.

I will only summarize a few lessons I have learned in the last few years. My spouse, the primary caretaker, has been prone to caregiver burnout. In hindsight, I can see things more clearly now. She has a minimizing, internalizing and avoidance tendencies but her history of grossly deficient self-care and excessive enmeshment and coddling especially her one grown daughter, but all of her family. This happened too much at the expense of normal self-care and friendships. This excessive investment in her family, given an anxious, selfless and enabling style (characteristic of her parents) is intertwined with low mood.

She became overwhelmed from caring for her mother (and sister) while working (an executive level position) and the burnout and stress that she minimized from the caregiving and her job undoubtedly contributed to her losing that high paying and irreplaceable job.

Internalizing and minimizing the primary problems at work contributed to a predictable job loss. While she was selflessly taking care of her mother, and sister, while attending too much to assisting her essentially unhelpful family members, as well as inability to modify self-induced stress, along with endless excuses and denial, this has had a deleterious effect on all areas of her life; albeit least on the caregiving part of it.

Although minimizing the burden of demands can initially prolong energy, it inevitably leads to personal deterioration in daily life. In our case, the job loss along with a very large debt default from her one daughter, both predictable but denied, caused stress both when we had conflict about even expressing predictable patterns and when they occurred and ruined a well-planned future that included early retirement for her (to escape the stresses of her job but in a financially smart way) and finances for spending retirement activities together, with very good predictability of of incurring future debt and being subjected to continuing stresses mostly from her absurdly spoiled and enabled younger daughter - with continued conflicts over her continued enablement.

I am nine years older and although still vibrant, when she retires, I will likely not be. Other factors re: her family also limit my ability to travel even after caregiving is relieved.

With focus on the effective efforts to promote healthy caregiving, we did implement some useful strategies. One strategy we employed while caregiving for her mom with dementia (and sister with chronic developmental problems) is under-reacting.

Under-reacting is a powerful general strategy that allows objective assessment of difficult situations and realities, but in a matter of fact manner of experience that delays and reduces negative emotional reactions and interpretations that can amplify distress and exhaustion. This allows primary focus on problem solving while bolstering hope versus the hopelessness that can extinguish problem solving efforts with exhaustion and pessimism before effective, incremental solutions can be found or worked on.

Another strategy specific to caregiving for persons with dementia is Validation Therapy. This involves an approach that seeks to interpret the often seemingly confused and illogical communications not as literal statements, but rather ones that have symbolic meaning. The meaning often represents remnants of previously important life issues/concerns, and most often unresolved ones. This approach replaces correction or literal reality confrontation in favor of validating the statements while exploring possible subjective underlying meaning. For example, rather than correcting mom with how dad is dead, we validated the feelings mom has of missing dad, like the ones she had for many years when dad was working long hours and not home much. Reassurance and understanding had a cathartic effect and helped prevent emotions from devolving into darker emotions and acting out.

Mom also always loved country music and singing, so we collaborated on how to compile a list of her favorite songs and made a playlist to play for her, including sometimes singing with her or playing guitar and prompting her to sing her favorite songs. As mom's condition worsened and abilities decreased, she would compulsively try to piddle while complaining of not doing anything useful. She had always had at least a mild level of baseline anxiety, was always active and had been a restless and compulsive cleaner who never tolerated sitting still or inactivity.

When we were able to problem solve an activity she was still capable of performing, we gave her silverware to polish.

Combined with lots of thanks and praise, her anxiety quieted and emotional improved. Also, even as she declined, she was still able sing along to some of her favorite songs,  so this became a staple activity.

Mom also had a historical pattern and habit of being irritable and mean, followed by feeling guilty and apologetic. She was also fairly defensive and prone to deny and challenge feedback. We found that highlighting how she hurt our feelings and/or expressing concern about why or what we might have done to make her feel bad (instead of negatively evaluating or trying to correct her behavior), we were able to help turn the switch from mean to apologetic, after which providing some reassurance and positive emotions usually stabilized her emotions. As mentioned above, the act of direct 24 hour caregiving has led to some modification and expansion of the Caregiver Survival Rules.

Recently, we were able to begin a search and were lucky to find a suitable and even highly desirable yet affordable residential Memory Care for mom, and adjustment has gone well, so our caregiving roles have changed dramatically. We are no longer direct 24 hour caregivers and are instead transitioning to more of a visiting relative role where quality interactions are predominant. As we are now in caregiver recovery mode, we are more actively processing what our next life phase will look like.

While I do not know what the next year will bring, I expect the survival rules will be updated and enhanced. Freshly evolving perspective and insights from the hands-on, raw experiences that came from daily caregiving have certainly supplemented understanding that was previously limited to only my consulting with and treating caregivers.

### Closing

The tips or advice offered in this chapter, and those available in videos, articles and books, including those offered at villamartelli.com, are powerful and can be very helpful. However, applying these insights and strategies can often be difficult to apply without guidance and encouragement.

Persisting with efforts until practice improves skills and makes using these strategies effective, habitual and less effortful, can be difficult. This is especially so for a caregiver who is distressed, emotionally drained, exhausted or burned out. In those cases, the sooner some kind of support is sought, the better. It is in the caregivers best interest, as well as that of the caregivee, to not minimize distress, fatigue or burnout and to seek support, starting with letting others know and seeking help.

In all cases, some level of assistance is helpful, and in many cases, more structured and professional guidance is beneficial or necessary. Support can range in degree and type. At the most basic level, family members who read available guides and provide encouragement and reinforcement can be helpful. For many, caregiver support groups are very helpful and these are available online and in local hospital, churches and other community settings.

For some to many caregivers, individual support from a counselor or psychologist experienced with assisting caregivers can be helpful or even necessary. It is in the best interest of the caregiver (and caregivee) to seek help, to let others know they need help, and to ask others help in problem solving how to get support, given their current circumstances.

For a more detailed review of available resources to assist caregivers, please visit: https://villamartelli.com/P_caregiverSurvival.pdf\

For an even more detailed and scholarly review of available caregiver resources, please feel free to email the me at the email address provided in the footer of that paper.

© Mike F. Martelli 2023 (with Yvette Prior)

*Time passed slowly...*

# CHAPTER EIGHT
## THERE'S NO RETURN TO SENDER
## BY ROBBIE CHEADLE

On the 30th of January 2006, at approximately 2:30 pm, my younger son, Michael, was born via caesarean section (C-Section), an operation to deliver the baby through a cut made in your abdomen and uterus.

My C-Section had been scheduled for 38-weeks' gestation as my gynaecologist did not want to risk my going into labour.

My older son, Gregory, was a complete breech presentation, his head was up under my ribs, both of his legs were bent, and his bottom and feet were closest to the birth canal. A complete breech presentation is a risk for the health of the baby as there is a greater chance of the umbilical cord forming a loop and coming out

144

through the cervix before the head, thereby cutting of the supply of oxygen to the baby. Greg had been delivered via a scheduled C-Section at 38 weeks and the operation had gone very smoothly. I was awake and had a spinal block, so I was able to hold him and breast feed him immediately.

My doctor did not think that 'virginal births after a caesarean section' (VBACs) were advisable and had recommended a C-Section birth for Michael. I had followed his advice. The method of delivery was not important to me, and I'd already had one C-Section.

I remember lying on the gurney in the theatre waiting area and crying. My husband, Terence, was there but his presence did not comfort me.

I was having a flashback of Greg's most recent operation. Greg had been born with a Hypospadias, a birth defect in boys in which the urethrae forms abnormally. At the age of two years and 11 months, he had already undergone major surgery three times. All three procedures had failed and a fourth was required. I had postponed the necessary surgery until the new baby was at least six months old.

*When I was six months pregnant with Michael, Greg underwent his third operation. I had concerns about Dr. Farmer performing this third operation after the failures of the previous two, but he told us that he had done his own research and held discussions with doctors at the Children's Hospital in Toronto, Canada. He felt confident that he was well prepared*

*for this third operation, and he convinced us to let*
*him perform the surgery.*

*The two weeks that followed Greg's third operation*
*were traumatic. At that time in my life I had no idea*
*what lay ahead for me and that I was to become an*
*expert on brittle asthma, superbugs, biofilms, sinus*
*problems, pulmonary embolism, venous sinus*
*thrombosis and high blood pressure. The operation*
*itself was no more eventful than the previous two, it*
*was afterwards. This time around, Greg developed*
*an allergic reaction to the catheter and his urine*
*started forming a sediment.*

*This reaction was most unfortunate and unexpected*
*and resulted in the catheter blocking on the Sunday*
*morning following the operation the previous*
*Friday. I noticed on the Sunday morning that the*
*catheter didn't seem to be filling up. I was worried.*
*I thought Greg wasn't drinking enough, and I was*
*very concerned about a bladder infection despite the*
*preventative antibiotic he was taking. As the*
*morning progressed, the catheter still didn't start*
*filling up and I started to get really concerned. Greg*
*was also very miserable and moaning. An hour*
*later, Greg was crying continuously, and the bag*
*was still empty.*

*Terence and I took Greg to the emergency room at*
*the hospital. Our child was beside himself by the*
*time we saw a doctor and so was I. I had been*
*carrying him around, crying and moaning for about*
*three hours and my back was aching miserably. I*

146

*was so worried I felt nauseous. The doctor was young and inexperienced, and he did not know what was wrong. He ended up phoning Dr. Farmer on his cell phone to get advice.*

*Dr. Farmer was out of town water skiing. He was at a dam about two hours' drive from the hospital. Dr. Farmer tried to explain to the young doctor how to unblock the catheter. Unfortunately, the Emergency Room doctor wasn't able to manage it. Greg's crying went on and on and eventually, in desperation, the young doctor called Dr. Farmer again. Dr. Farmer said that he would come. We had to wait a further two hours for him to drive from the dam.*

*That awful two hours seemed never ending. I was frantic in case something terrible happened to my son. Being in a hospital didn't help at all as no-one was able to assist us. When Dr. Farmer eventually arrived, he resolved the situation very quickly. He used a syringe to unblock the catheter and the urine began to flow. Greg was given a painkiller and soon quietened down and went to sleep. We took him home and we all went to bed early, completely exhausted by the events of the day.*

*Later that night, Greg woke up, moaning and uncomfortable. I checked the bag and the urine was flowing so I thought he was just upset and reacting to the trauma of the day. I sat up with him for two hours that night, reading to him and cuddling him until he eventually went back to sleep. The following morning, I undressed him to wash him down as he couldn't bath with the catheter inserted. To my horror, I saw that the tube from the catheter to the bag had pulled up under the plaster that was holding it in position. My poor baby couldn't straighten his body without pulling on the catheter which was very uncomfortable and painful. He was walking bent over like an old man. I loosened the plaster and lengthened the tube so that the catheter wasn't pulling. My heart felt tight and painful in my chest as I cuddled my little boy. It's so hard to see your child struggling and be so stupid and not be able to help.*

*On Tuesday morning, the catheter blocked again. This time I did not mess around. I put Greg in the car and drove straight to Dr. Farmer's rooms. He saw us within fifteen minutes and unblocked the catheter again. I felt terrible that the catheter had blocked again, and it seemed likely to me that it would block again over the course of the remaining ten day recovery period. I asked Dr. Farmer to show me how to unblock the catheter with the syringe.*

*He showed me slowly and I practiced a few times to make sure I was competent. I picked up my son and the syringe and we went home. The catheter continued to block every couple of days and each time I managed to successfully unblock it. I felt much more empowered once I was able to unblock it myself and react to Greg's symptoms before they became too intense.*

*I found out later how dangerous a blocked catheter can be as the urine that collects and can't be passed can wash up into your kidneys and cause a kidney infection. I am very grateful that Greg did not experience any complications that were worse than the severe discomfort and pain.*
*I hoped that this operation would be successful, and I would never have to experience this horror again. A month later we discovered that the third operation had also failed.*

The anaesthetist was most concerned about my tears. He asked me why I was worried.
"I'm scared this baby will have something wrong with him?" I answered.
"Don't worry," the anaesthetist consoled me after I'd shared a summary of Greg's history. "Lightening rarely strikes twice. Everything will be fine with this baby."
But he was wrong; it wasn't.

## The Beginning

In the beginning everything seemed fine. Michael was born weighing 3.1 kilograms and had an Apgar score of ten out of ten. Apgar is a test given to new-borns soon after birth. This test checks the baby's heart rate, muscle tone, and other signs to see if extra medical care or emergency care is needed.

Gregory's Apgar score had been nine out of ten. He'd peed all over the paediatrician while his Apgar score check was being performed, resulting in immediate identification of his medical condition.

While we were in the hospital, everything was easier for me with Michael. He latched and breast fed easily, and I managed nappy and clothing changes much better than I had when Greg was born. The second time around was a comparative breeze.

I was lonely in the hospital as I didn't have many visitors. My mom and dad were looking after Greg and my husband was working so he could take his paternity leave when the baby and I came home. Most of my friends had their own small children or babies to look after so they weren't available for hospital visits. I asked my gynaecologist if we could be discharged early. He said it was up to the paediatrician.

The paediatrician, Dr. Dream, was happy with Michael's health and feeding. She agreed to discharge us after 48 hours instead of the usual 72 hours.

I went home and introduced Greg to his new baby brother. Greg did not welcome Michael. He lay on the bed on our first night home, kicking and screaming. Greg wanted me to bath him and put him to bed and I couldn't because I was feeding the baby.

"What about me?" he sobbed.

The days passed and everyone settled into the new routine. Greg was mollified if I read books to him while I breastfed the baby. We read up to seven short children's books a day.

I used a pram a lot more for Michael than I had for Greg. The baby would sleep in the pram in the room where I was busy doing chores or playing with Greg.

Everything seemed to be going so well for the first two weeks of Michael's life. I had developed mastitis in the left breast after Greg was born. It was incredibly painful, far worse than the site of the C-Section. I didn't want to take antibiotics, so I used cabbage leaves to help with the inflammation. I also used a homeopathic remedy. The two interventions worked, and I was able to continue breast feeding Greg for a bit longer.

I have terrible scarring because of the mastitis and the radiologist comments on it every time I have a mammogram. I call them my battle scars. I also hardly slept for the two weeks while the mastitis raged, and I was stressed and exhausted as a result.
One ordinary afternoon when Michael was three weeks old, I checked on him sleeping in the pram. He was blue. He'd stopped breathing. I snatched him up and he awoke and started screaming.

I was terrified. I packed both children and my mom into the car and went straight to our paediatrician's office. After examining the baby, Dr. Dream said he had bronchiolitis and needed to be admitted into hospital. Bronchiolitis is a common viral infection among infants that causes the airways (bronchioles) in the lungs to become narrow, which makes breathing difficult. Greg wasn't allowed into the paediatric ward, so he and Mom had to sit outside in the small waiting area while Michael was admitted and a drip was inserted. I called Terence and asked him to come and fetch them. It caused me a lot of extra stress knowing they were sitting just outside the door. In retrospect, I should have left them both at home.

For three nights and days, I stayed in the hospital with Michael. He slept in an oxygen tent and received antibiotics through a drip. He also had cortisone. My husband and Mom looked after Greg at home. It was a horrible time and I felt guilty. I'd taken Michael to the birthday party of one of Greg's friends and suspected that he'd picked up a virus from one of the other toddler party goers.

To make matters worse, my father-in-law, who had been ailing for some time, died unexpectedly. I didn't see him before he passed away. Terence and I had gone to visit him in the Intensive Care Unit (ICU) at Milpark Hospital before Michael was born. The nurses wouldn't let me into the ICU. I was eight months pregnant and there was a risk I could pick up an infection from one of the patients.

I ended up sitting outside on a chair in the passage for 45 minutes.

I spent most of the three days in the hospital alone with Michael. My husband was supporting his mother and sister and helping them with the funeral arrangements.

On day four, Michael and I were discharged with a bag of medication including saline and a decongestant spray containing Oxymetazoline Hydrochloride to clear obstructions in his nasal passages, and cortisone. The cortisone had to be mixed with a saline solution and administered through a nebuliser which turned the liquid into a fine mist for him to breath via a plastic mask.

We purchased a nebuliser, but it wasn't anything like the quick machine in the hospital. It took me 40 minutes to nebulise him, and it had to be done six times, every four hours, in a 24-hour period. Michael was breastfeeding and Dr. Dream was determined this was necessary for his immune system, so I was getting up twice during the night, injecting one centimetre of saline into each nostril followed by a decongestant, breast feeding for 80 minutes, nebulizing for 40 minutes, and sleeping for two hours if I was lucky, before repeating the whole cycle. This continued for three weeks until Michael's six-week check-up with Dr. Dream.

I was exhausted. Driving was awful and it was only Michael's screaming in the car that kept me from dozing off. Michael was a monster in the car. I have subsequently realised his crying and screaming were due to his sinus and breathing issues.

At the time it was unexpected. Greg had loved the car and we would often go for a drive in the middle of the night to get him to sleep. Greg had his days and nights confused and would sleep all day and be awake half the night. He slept through the night for the first time when he was nine years old.

The air conditioner was on full, blasting me with cold air as I drove the short distance from home to the hospital. Michael's continuous crying wound me up and my nerves felt stretched and tight. I retrospect, at least I knew he was breathing.

Dr. Dream's check-up was thorough.
"This baby's got the narrowest nasal passages I've ever
seen," she declared at the end of it. I was given a script
for *Flixanase* nasal drops which contain corticosteroids
to clear nasal obstructions and reduce inflammation.
"The baby is mouth breathing and that is not usual for
newborns. This medication will help him breath through
his nose which is better for his long-term health."

Our next hospitalisation was in May. At four-months old,
Michael was adorable with a huge smile and a delightful
giggle, especially when I washed his neck. He had been
gaining weight well and everything seemed fine, so his
second bout of bronchiolitis came as a shock.

We spent another three days in the paediatric ward. It
turned out that this time, Michael contracted the illness
from Greg who had contracted croup at playgroup. Greg
also spent a few days in the hospital on intravenous
antibiotics, cortisone and being nebulised.

After the two boys had been discharged from hospital, I
took Greg out of playgroup. He'd been going three
mornings a week to give me a bit of relief and so that he
could socialise with children his age. He stayed at home
with Michael and I for the next two months.

I went back to work in August, the last month of the
South African winter, on a five-hour a day contract. I'd
been paid in full for the first four months of my maternity
leave and taken another two months as unpaid leave. In

terms of my maternity contract, I had to work for the firm
for twelve months or pay back my maternity leave on a
pro-rata basis.

In October 2006, on the advice of a new paediatric
specialist surgeon, Dr. Roy, Greg underwent surgery for
the fourth time. This procedure was more successful from
a reconstructive perspective but resulted in extensive scar
tissue which narrowed his urethrae and caused one
bladder infection after another.

It was a dreadful time with Greg on continuous
antibiotics. After the fourth bladder infection, Greg was
put on a prophylactic antibiotic to prevent the infections.
It didn't work because his urethrae was too narrow and
the urine collected in his bladder, becoming infected. His
urine came out in a thin stream, but like a high-pressure
spray.

Michael was also continuously sick over the course of the
spring and summer, but he wasn't hospitalised again until
March 2007, when he was 14 months old. March is the
beginning of autumn in the Southern Hemisphere and
fraught with 'changing season' colds and flu. Between
March and June of 2007, Michael was admitted into
hospital twice with bronchitis.

In desperation, I handed in my notice at the beginning of
June. This was two months before the end of my
maternity leave lock-in period, so I had to pay back two
months of salary to the firm. At the time, Michael was
sixteen months old, and Greg was 4 years old.

I found another job that allowed me more flexibility and to work from home. My mother was having some health issues due to arthritis in both her hips, so her ability to help me with the boys was limited.

My new role was more complicated than my previous job and it was more stressful and demanding as a result, but I didn't like having to leave my sick children at home with a caregiver, so I made it work.

I worked late into the night every weekday and grabbed opportunities to work over weekends if Michael slept during the day. Greg slept every afternoon until he was three. He also slept a lot during the period of bladder infections due to his poor health. Greg didn't sleep well at night and woke me up at least twice every night.

Michael never slept much during the day, but he slept very well at night. Usually from about 6.30pm until 6am. That changed over time, of course, but it helped for the first six months of my new job.

In hindsight, I don't know how I did it as I worked night after night, often for three or four weeks on the trot without a single night off. I was permanently tired, but I could spend a lot more time with my little ones.

Greg continued to suffer from bladder infections. Dr. Roy tried to solve the problem of his constricted urethrae by performing stretches to break down the scar tissue and open the urethrae. By June 2008, Greg had undergone six of these minor procedures under anaesthetic. Following each procedure, he would be fine for about three weeks

and then a new bladder infection would start.
"I want to try something different," Dr. Roy said in July.
"Let's do the urethrae stretches weekly for the four
weeks of August and see if that will get rid of the scar
tissue build up permanently."

There being no other viable options, I agreed, and Greg
had the four procedures. At four and a half years old,
Greg was aware of his repeated hospitalisations and was
highly traumatised. The symptoms of Obsessive
Compulsive Disorder ("OCD") he had started displaying
at the age of two and half escalated. His compulsions at
this age manifested as repeated requests for reassurance
in respect of everything he did, but particularly with
regards to his health. I wrote this poem at the time which
describes how this period was for me.

**Internal Anxieties**
As anxieties rise,
reassurance he'll seek,
he's wary of lies,
told glib and sleek.

I watch and see,
the struggle unfold,
he's part of me,
it's hard to behold.

His life is fear,
he'll furtively wait,
what will appear,
to seal his fate.

His giver of life,
to her he turns,
to calm the strife,
that internally churns.

What takes place,
inside his head,
some thoughts, like lice,
others molten lead.

Which will endure,
he must decide,
the other obscure,
and strongly override.

Unfortunately, Dr. Roy's attempts to break down the scar tissue failed, and Greg was diagnosed with another chronic bladder infection in October 2007, despite being on a daily prophylactic antibiotic. The combination of repeated anaesthetics, bladder infections and antibiotics resulted in chronic fatigue syndrome. If I took Greg out to the shops after school, he'd fall asleep in the shopping cart. He slept for three or four hours after school every afternoon.

Michael was also sick all the time. In early spring, I took him back to Dr. Dream. He sounded like a truck going up a hill when he breathed. This time, he was diagnosed with asthma and given an inhaler as well as more cortisone and antibiotics. At eighteen months old, he'd been on twelve courses of cortisone and antibiotics.

Dr. Roy was at a loss as to what to do to improve Greg's

health. He reached out to the Children's Hospital in Montreal for advice. In early November he called me to a meeting at this rooms to discuss the way forward.
"We need to reconstruct the entire urethrae," Dr. Roy advised. The tissue for the reconstruction will need to be taken from the inside of his mouth. That is the only area on the body with sufficient tissue of the correct texture and consistency for this specific reconstruction process."

I must have looked horrified as he hastened to add: "We will have to put Greg into an induced coma for seven days after the surgery to allow the inside of his mouth to heal. He will not feel the pain."
What a horrible procedure to have to put your child through. Greg was not yet five years old and he'd already undergone 14 procedures under general anaesthetic.

The professor at the Children's Hospital in Montreal diagnosed Greg with a condition called Balanitis Xerotica Obliterans, a chronic penile skin condition that effects the foreskin, glans penis and urethrae. There was no cure other than to replace the effected tissue.

Given this diagnosis, there were no other options. The procedure was scheduled for early December and the professor from Montreal and a colleague of his would participate via video conferencing.

Dr. Roy came out of the operating theatre after fifty minutes. Terence and I were waiting in the theatre sitting room even though the procedure was expected to last four to five hours. He was smiling as he came over to us. "We didn't need to do the skin graft and reconstruction surgery," he said. We removed a chunk of scar tissue that was obstructing the end of the urethrae and we believe that will do the trick.""

I was filled with thankfulness that this dreaded procedure had ended up being so much shorter and simpler. The site where the tissue had been removed was small and not very noticeable. It would heal up well and no-one would even know it was there except us and Greg.

Christmas was a happy one with both boys doing relatively well, health wise.

In April, Dr. Roy told us he was immigrating to America. His practice was being taken over by his younger colleague, Dr. Love. Greg's case was handed over to Dr. Love, who although rather arrogant and overly self-confident, was a competent doctor.

Dr. Love showed Greg and I how to do urethrae stretches at home. We started with our new home programme which removed the need for urethrae stretches under anaesthetic.

**No diagnosis.**

Michael, on the other hand, was sick all the time. Every few weeks he caught a cold which escalated into sinusitis. He was on a constant stream of antibiotics and cortisone.

In the lead up to his fourth birthday, Michael started getting eye infections. Initially, Dr. Dream treated these with antibiotics and eye drops, but they kept coming back. It was always his left eye that started swelling and oozing.

Every time Dr. Dream saw him, she would look up his nose and say: "Wall to wall snot and so much inflammation."

On Dr. Dream's recommendation, we took Michael to an ophthalmologist who did a thorough examination of his eyes and tested him for various eye diseases. All the tests came back negative, but the eye infections persisted. Finally, Dr. Dream suggested he see an otolaryngologists or ear, nose, and throat specialist (ENT). I booked an appointment with an older ENT at Olivedale Mediclinic. This was not our usual clinic, but Dr. Dream recommended Dr. Bird, so I took him there, despite the clinic being much less conveniently located for me.

The appointment with Dr. Bird was a waste of money and time. He checked Michael for the usual childhood ailments, adenoids, and fluid in the middle ear, and proclaimed there was nothing wrong with him. "Tough love," was his solution to Michael's continuous apathy, illnesses, and reluctance to go to school. "You must make him go to school as there is nothing wrong with him."

Dr. Bird never did a CT scan or checked for any issues with the sinuses.

Halfway through this fifth year, Michael started getting terrible stomach pain. Every day he complained about his sore stomach. I took him to Dr. Dream, and she sent him for a plethora of tests for various ailments.

Dr. Dream did all the blood tests herself. I had to hold Michael still while she filled the little vials with blood. Following a few bad experiences with inexperienced nurses attempting to take his blood, Michael was very difficult and screamed and howled for the entire duration of the appointment.

All the tests came back negative.
Finally, he was sent for a sonar. The radiologist spent a lot of time with him. Eventually, after a multitude of changes to his position, she finished and told us her report would go directly to Dr. Dream.
Later that day, Dr. Dream called.
"The radiologist has identified a mass in Michael stomach. You need to take him for a CT scan."

The CT scan also took ages. It is very difficult to get a four-year-old to stay completely still long enough for the pictures to be taken. The radiographer persisted and the scan was eventually completed to his satisfaction. Once again, the report was sent directly to the doctor.

Dr. Dream called us later that afternoon and asked both me and my husband to come and see her the following morning.

"Michael has a tumour in this stomach," Dr. Dream explained. "He needs to have an operation to remove the mass and a biopsy will be done to test for cancer."

The doctor didn't say it explicitly, but she clearly thought Michael had cancer. Before we left, she offered us her blood if Michael required a blood transfusion at any time.

The procedure to remove the mass would be performed by Dr. Love. I was grateful that at least I knew Dr. Love and trusted his competency as a doctor. The operation was scheduled for the following week as there was a long weekend ahead.

It was the worst long weekend I've ever experienced. I couldn't eat or sleep for worrying about the operation and the possibility of cancer. I was so distracted that when I bathed the two boys that Friday evening, they pulled on me to get my attention, and I fell into the bath.
My sister and her then boyfriend were visiting at the time. It was incredibly difficult to try and entertain them when my mind was in such a bad place.

The time passed slowly, but it did pass and on the scheduled day, Terence and I took Michael to the hospital. The pre-hospitalisation process was an ordeal as Michael couldn't have anything to eat after 10pm the previous evening. He couldn't drink anything after 6am in the morning and our hospital check-in was at 12pm. It is not easy dealing with a stressed out, hungry, and thirsty four-year-old.

Naturally, Michael was clinging to me like a limpet and wouldn't let me out of his sight so I couldn't eat or drink anything either.

The lists for operations go strictly in order of the patients age with babies being first and adults last. Michael was third on the list and the theatre called for him at 2pm. Due to his young age, one parent was allowed to go into the theatre with the child and remain until the anaesthetic had been administered and the child was unconscious. Michael wanted me, so I had to go into the theatre changing room and put on a full set of theatre overalls. My shoes were covered by disposable theatre boots and a disposable hairnet covered my hair.

Michael and I waited outside the theatre until the nurses came to take his gurney into the theatre. I followed and assumed my position holding his hand, while the anaesthetist administered the sleeping gas that smelled like strawberries.

Putting my children under anaesthetic is always traumatic for me as there is the small risk that something could go wrong. One of my sister's school friends died under anaesthetic during a small tonsillectomy. That knowledge has followed me all my life and added to my stress related to my children's procedures.

When Michael was asleep, I left the theatre and went to the coffee shop with Terence to get something to eat and drink. The operation was expected to take between 2 and 3 hours. I couldn't eat anything and felt quite nauseous smelling all the greasy food, but it passed the time. After 90 minutes, I made Terence get the bill and went back up to the theatre to wait for the doctor. I was in such a state of agitation, I couldn't even sit down, but rather paced up and down the short piece of corridor outside the theatre doors.

About 45 minutes later, the doctor came out to speak to us. Everything had gone well, and Michael was in recovery. The mass was a hugely enlarged lymph node that was wrapped around the main artery in his stomach. The doctor had removed half of the node but had left the other half as it was too risky to try and remove it.

"The remaining half will shrivel up and be reabsorbed back into his body," Dr. Love said. "I have sent a piece of the node away for testing at the laboratory, but I don't believe it is cancerous. It doesn't have the look of malignant tissue."

Michael had to stay overnight in the hospital. I stayed with him, sleeping, or rather dozing, on a fold out sleeper chair. I remember his small frame in the hospital bed. His face was as white as the surrounding pillow and sheets. He experienced a lot of pain and called for me several times during the night to cuddle him and hold his hand until he fell back into a fitful sleep.

I wrote this poem that night:

**The Hospital**

Oh, how I hate the hospital
what a dreary and austere place
I hate it more and more each time
it raises its clinically sterile face.

The white noise is just awful,
children, crying through the night,

it's meant to do the opposite,
but it sucks out all the hope and light.

It hurts to see his dear, little face,
on the pillow, clean and white,
the fact their colours match,
makes it a really horrible sight.

If I had to describe the hospital
I would call it a modern version of Hell,
just being in this cesspit of illness,
is enough to make me feel unwell.

There was another small boy in the hospital during our stay. He was younger than Michael, I guessed he was about 3 years old. Neither of his parents stayed with him in the hospital overnight, in fact, I never saw either parent once during Michael and my time on the ward.

The boy cried and cried. I remember the nurse carrying him around, his head buried in her neck and his small shoulders heaving with sobs. I wondered how anyone could leave such a young child, clearly very ill, all alone in the hospital. It made me feel sad. I never found out what was wrong with that boy, but he was carried about continuously by the nursing staff who were exceptionally kind and caring towards him.

The following morning, Dr. Love and Dr. Dream came to see Michael and at 12pm we were discharged.
Dr. Love's belief that the tumour was not malignant was comforting, but I still worried for the entire 5 days until Dr. Dream called me with the results of the biopsy. When

she said it was not cancerous, I burst into tears and sobbed my heart out. It was such a huge relief.

The removal of the lymph did help Michael's stomach pain, but we continued our cycles of respiratory and other illnesses.

A few months later in the spring, Michael got very sick again and spent three days in hospital. By this time, I had learned to skip the emergency room and just take him straight to the Paediatric Ward at the hospital. We would wait there for Dr. Dream to do her rounds and then she would see Michael. After a previous disaster with the removal of the drip when the nurse forgot to clamp it and Michael's blood sprayed everywhere when she pulled it out traumatising him and me, Dr. Dream now put in and took out the drip.

During this stay in the hospital, we met a woman whose daughter suffered from recurring bouts of pneumonia. The little girl, a sweet little thing with blonde curly hair and large blue eyes, had contracted flu when she was young. The young mother admitted that neither she nor her young husband and realised how serious their child's illness was and they had not taken her to the doctor until she was so ill her oxygen levels had dropped to 65 and her lips were blue. The girl had pneumonia and it had caused serious damage to her lungs. Subsequent to that hospitalisation, five years previously, every time the child caught a cold, her lungs filled up with fluid and she ended up in hospital in an oxygen tent.

Michael was not recovered when we left the hospital and

was still receiving an intravenous antibiotic through the drip, but Dr. Dream had agreed he was sufficiently recovered to go home, and he could be an outpatient for the remaining four days of his treatment.

Each day, I drove Michael to the hospital, and we spent approximately four hours in the treatment room attached to the Paediatric Ward while he received his intravenous antibiotic. He was such a good boy and I used to read to him for a couple of hours and then play board games with him.

Michael developed a passion for Enid Blyton's *Famous Five* books during this time. He begged me to read them to him over and over again. He had a particular affinity for *Five Go Off in a Caravan*. I became heartily sick of that story and eventually resorted to acquiring all the Famous Five stories as audio books. Michael would lie on the couch in the family room listing to these audio books for hours while I worked.

A week after the antibiotic course completed and the drip had been removed, Michael had another check up with Dr. Dream. She wasn't happy with his oxygen levels which were in the low 80s despite the huge doses of cortisone, intravenous antibiotic, heavy doses of asthma medication and Flixanase nasal drops.

"Michael needs to see a paediatric pulmonologist, someone who specialises in asthma in children."

Dr. Dream recommended Dr. James. I knew Dr. James as he was the attending paediatrician when Gregory was

born. He was the doctor who identified his medical
condition. He had seen Gregory two or three times after
his birth for the usual check-ups and I had elected to
change to Dr. Dream.

Dr. James was an extremely odd man who kept us
waiting for hours and hours in his room for each
appointment. He took on every specialised or emergency
medical case that came his way and did a lot of *pro bono*
charity work. I was not against the *pro bono* work but
sitting in a doctor's waiting room for seven or eight hours
with a sick small child is difficult.

I tried to go prepared for Michael's appointments with
Dr. James. I took along books to read to him as well as
his Leapfrog pad. These activities did work as a diversion
for Michael for a while, but it was a very tedious wait in
a dreary waiting room full of sick children and desperate
looking moms. The doctor would flit in and out, seeing
patients, in between rushing off to deliver babies and deal
with emergencies.

Dr. James could never say no to any case. During one
visit, while we were waiting, we saw a small girl who
was a burn victim. She had clearly had skin grafts and
cosmetic repair work done to her face and hands. It was
very sad to see this small child sitting there quietly, her
hands swathed in bandages and her hair all shaved off.
She was very small boned and her dress, although very
pretty, was far too big for her. She was obviously one of
his *pro bono* cases.

I have never forgotten that child and thought it was

admirable that the doctor assisted with that sort of highly complex case, but I still found his behaviour to be a trial at the time and thought it was rude of him to expect his paying patients to wait for so long.

When we finally managed to see the doctor, I always felt pressured to get Michael's latest symptoms and stories told as quickly as possible so that the appointment could finish before the doctor was summonsed and disappeared into the bowels of the hospital for another hour or two. I thought that was a bit unfair on Michael and me.

Dr. James had frizzy greying hair and wore an old-fashioned white doctor's coat with a stethoscope around his neck. He was the very picture of an old-fashioned, kindly doctor. The sort of country doctor you read about in books like *What Katy Did* and *Pollyanna*. This initial pleasant picture soon changed, however, and I personally found him to be very irritating. He mumbled to himself all the time, commenting on my child and his condition under his breath but not actually coming out with anything and telling me what his thoughts or concerns were.

It was Dr. James who told me that Michael's asthma was brittle. This meant that it was not well controlled despite the high levels of asthma medication he was taking. His asthma medication doses were so high, the medical aid said it was an adult dose and would only pay for the medication every second month. I was slightly resentful about the medical aid's attitude at the time, not really because of the expense, but because I felt it insinuated that I was over-medicating my child. This was not the case. Michael been under Dr. Dream's care ever since he was born and she had prescribed this dosage level for him, as nothing else worked.

Dr. James did help Michael a little bit by giving him an additional inhaler to support the primary inhaler. This second inhaler did seem to ease his breathing marginally, but this small difference was only noticeable after several months of treatment. I think that Dr. James found Michael to be an annoying case as none of his suggestions made a significant difference to Michael's poorly controlled asthma. Dr. James was used to winning and he didn't cope with failure well.

Each visit was the same, with Michael undergoing a battery of tests while the doctor muttered and mumbled under his breath about brittle asthma.

The doctor had a fun test which involved blowing hard into a thick tube connected to a computer. This action caused a computer-generated bowling ball to roll down the bowling alley. If you exhaled with average strength for your age, then all the bowling balls would fall over. Michael rarely knocked over more than five or six.

Dr. James also did some tests which determined that Michael had no natural immunity, and this was why he got so sick all the time. Dr. James sent Michael to see an endocrinologist, a specialised doctor who treats hormone imbalances in the body, as some of the tests suggested potential thyroid problems. Fortunately, the tests performed by the endocrinologist came back negative, so one theory for his medical condition was eliminated.

After a year of appointments that took up my entire day and yielded few results, I took Michael back to Dr. Dream. Based on the results of the numerous tests Dr. James had administered, together with the results from the endocrinologist, Michael's vaccinations were all redone and he was also vaccinated against pneumococcal polysaccharide vaccine which helps prevent pneumonia.

The following year, Michael turned six and started his Reception year at school. By August, Michael had missed over twenty school days due to illness and Dr. Dream decided to send him to another specialist ENT for further testing.

**Some success at last.**

Dr. Dream made the appointment with Dr. Mac herself. "I called him and gave him Michael's history," she said. I thought that was kind of her. Michael's medical history was the size of a telephone directory.

Our appointment was on a Thursday. Dr. Mac's rooms were packed with sick children and their parents, but we only waited three hours which was bearable.

Dr. Mac had a lot of fascinating pieces of equipment which he used for the examination. He inserted a tiny camera at the end of a narrow tube up his nose and into his sinuses. "I need him to have a CT scan," Dr. Mac said after his examination. "It is the only way I can really see what is happening in his sinuses."

Dr. Mac gave me the forms for the CT scan, and I made another appointment for one week later to discuss the findings and the next steps. "He has no drainage pathway for the maxillary and ethmoid sinuses on the left and the drainage pathway on the right is very narrow. As a result, the mucus in his maxillary and ethmoid sinuses is trapped and keeps getting infected. The eye infections he is experiencing are a result of the infection travelling to the tissue at the back of the eye."

I nodded, this made sense to me, and I wondered why none of the other doctors had thought of it.

"Michael needs to have surgery to correct these problems. The surgery will involve the creation of a new opening from his maxillary sinus, the sinus cavity behind his left cheek, to his nose so that the mucus can drain. This procedure is called Caldwell Luc surgery. He does have a drainage pathway on the right so I will perform Functional Endoscopic Sinus Surgery on that side. This surgery will widen the drainage passages between his nose and his right sinuses. Excess bone and infected tissue will be removed during this process."

"What is the success rate for sinus operations?" I asked. I was cautious after the three surgery failures we had experienced with Gregory's surgery.
"Sinus surgery has a high success rate with rare complications," Dr. Mac reassured me. "The surgery should stop the eye infections and reduce Michael's sinus problems. Sinus surgery doesn't always cure sinusitis. It is part of a treatment plan and Michael will need to continue with other medications into the future."

Terence and I agreed to the surgery. There was no other option.

The surgery was scheduled for a Wednesday. The operation would be at 2pm in the afternoon, and once again we went through the no eating or drinking routine. At six years old, Michael tolerated the pre-operation requirements better and I could at least explain to him that he couldn't eat so he wouldn't vomit during the operation.

Once again Michael asked me to accompany him into the theatre and I went through the drill of changing into the hospital overalls and putting on the disposable shoes and hair net. I waited with Michael in the theatre waiting area as I had done so many times with Gregory.

While we were waiting, a gurney was wheeled into the waiting area. The small figure in the bed was swathed in bandages. The mother was going into theatre with the child, and she looked shell shocked. I remember her dark eyes surrounded by dark bruised looking flesh and the tight drawn look on her face.

I wondered what was wrong with the child. She looked like a burn victim.

Just then, the anaesthetist and Dr. Mac came to speak to Michael and me. A few minutes later, I was following Michael's gurney into the theatre. The anaesthetic procedure didn't take long and within fifteen minutes I had left my sleeping child in the doctors' care, changed back into my own clothes, and gone downstairs to have coffee with Terence. It was our normal hospital routine. I remember seeing several people waiting in the theatre waiting area outside the sliding doors. It was only later I realised they were the relatives of the child with the bandages.

Unable to eat much, I drank a cappuccino and nibbled on a biscuit. Terence managed to eat breakfast, which at least filled up some of the dreadful waiting time. After whiling away about 90 minutes, we went back upstairs to the theatre waiting room.

The waiting room was empty except for the parents of the child with the bandages. I recognised the mother at once. Her face was white and strained and her eyes held a haunted look. The father was sitting and staring into space.

I smiled at her and sat down. After a while, she asked me why I was there. It has always amazed me how complete strangers strike up intimate conversations about their children and lives in hospital situations. I have experienced it many times subsequently to this operation. After explaining about Michael and his medical history, I asked her about her child.

"Fatima had a cold," the mother explained. "I gave her some Painaway syrup (fictional name) for the pain and fever. I was careful to give her the recommended 2.5 ml as she is only 18 months old and small for her age. She had a massive allergic reaction to one of the ingredients in the medication and her entire body and face, even her scalp under her hair, came up in terrible blisters as if she'd been burned."

Horrified, I didn't even know what to say to this poor woman, but worse was to come.

"The allergic reaction didn't only affect her skin," she continued, "the blisters extended to her lips, mouth, throat, and urethrae. The infection spread to her blood and has resulted in shock and some of her organs have started to fail."

"I am so sorry," I said. The words sounded pathetic, but I had nothing else to offer her. The father continued to sit, staring at nothing. His face was an unreadable mask.

I later learned that the little girl, Fatima, had Stevens-Johnson syndrome, a rare and serious disorder of the skin and mucous membranes.

Just then, Dr. Mac appeared at the door and beckoned for us to follow him. Standing in the hall outside the theatre doors, he told us that the procedure was finished. He had created a new drainage pathway for Michael on the left and opened the right pathway too. He was confident about the success of the operation and expected that the quality of Michael's life would improve significantly.

A short while later, I donned my hairnet and shoe coverings and went into recovery. Michael is aggressive and angry when he comes around from a surgical procedure and the nurses liked me to be there to help calm him down.

There were no issues with this first sinus procedure and no unusual bleeding or swelling. As a result, at 8pm that evening, Michael was discharged from hospital, and we went home.

The last few months of Michael Reception school year went well, and he didn't contract sinusitis or bronchitis. We had a lovely Christmas, and I started the year thinking that everything would go well for Michael in Grade one.

Unfortunately, my hopes were quickly dashed in the new year when Michael got very sick in March and missed two weeks of school. Dr. Mac recommended a sinus drain to deal with the acute congestion he was experiencing. This operation ended up being the first of a further 20 procedures Michael has undertaken to date, between the ages of 7 and 17.

I have spent many hours sitting in hospitals with one or other of my sons and have become very practiced at passing the time. I take my laptop with me and work while I wait. This helps me to focus on something quite different from their illnesses and pushes the anxiety from my mind.

I have also come to realise over the past 20 years, during which my children have had 40 medical procedures between them, that my lot is not that bad. There are many parents out there who face even worse medical conditions and procedures and the prognosis of many of the children who spend a lot of time in hospital is worse than for my two boys.

Michael was tested for cystic fibrosis, a hereditary and life-threatening disorder that damages the lungs and digestive system. The results were negative, and I am extremely grateful for that. During our many hospitalisations I got to know the repeat patients and several of them were cystic fibrosis patients. Treatment of the condition eases symptoms and reduces complications but it cannot be cured. The average life expectancy for cystic fibrosis patients in the developed world is between 42 and 50 years.

Michael has travelled a long road between this first operation and the most recent one in November 2022. He had blood tests recently and he will be seeing a rheumatologist in June this year (2023). The new ENT, Dr. Kind, and I are hopeful that no further invasive medical intervention will be need until after he finishes school next year (end of 2024).

I would like to leave you with this haiku that I wrote about my children:

> When loved ones sicken
> We transfer our life essence
> From ourselves to them

© Robbie Cheadle 2023

*Inspiration and consolation...*

# CHAPTER NINE
## NUMBERS LIE
## BY LAUREN SCOTT

Keri stares at the gold, shiny facade that draws her closer as though it holds magnetic force, and she is the magnet. The sun ascends in the clear sky, and the temperature is mild. Monday arrives with another weekend in the rearview mirror. She recalls the piles of work that camouflage her desk at the office but first things first.

Keri sheds her pajamas and pulls the blue scrunchie out of her hair, letting the brown mane cascade over her shoulders. Coffee can wait. She steps on the scale, lifting her left foot onto the gold. Her right foot follows as she inhales, holding her breath. She knows the white, luminescent numbers flickering three times will steer her mood like a pendulum to the left or right. Only occasionally does the pendulum stay centered. Once she steps off and her feet touch the cool tile floor, will she feel like clicking her heels in the air? Or will the flickering numbers cause her to feel down about herself? The courage to snub its magnetic lure stays in hiding.

She still cringes when she peruses old albums with photos of her as a young chubby girl. The memory of her ten-year-old self in the hospital after having her tonsils removed causes her stomach to somersault. Following the tonsillectomy, she rested in the recovery room with other children. A blonde-haired boy about her same age wore a wicked grin just before the words slid from his tongue, "Hey, fatso!" Those three syllables caused her to crumble into the white sterile bed sheets. Maybe they sparked her insecurities. Or perhaps the childhood chubbiness that dogged her footsteps into adulthood goaded the insecurities to surface.

Keri's best friend is her doting mom, who enjoys showing love through her cooking. What could be better than a homestyle meal? Keri distinctly recalls the wonderful dinners and desserts her mom made from scratch with intoxicating aromas and delicious flavors. But she finds it hard to believe that a young child would say, "I don't want the cookie, Mommy. I want a carrot instead." Thus, the sweets and treats offered to Keri when she was little compounded the pounds. Her mom isn't responsible, though. Keri has been an adult for too long to play the ignorant card. She knows which foods make a healthy choice and which foods deliver comfort. Some provide both, but most land in their respective columns.

The battle of losing unwanted pounds remains perpetual.

A truckload of willpower needs to pull right up to the curb in front of Keri's house, which it has in the past. But keeping the weight off requires a lifestyle change. *I can't do the same thing and expect different results.* It's no easy feat to grip self-discipline. It's like trying to hold a fish.

Keri pads to the kitchen and scrounges up something to munch whenever her feet feel like dancing or circumstances warrant nail biting. She could slap a yellow sticky note on her forehead with emotional eater written in Sharpie. Whatever the emotion, food tempts her like a dangling carrot to a starving rabbit. But she doesn't crave carrots. Carrots aren't an issue. Sugar is the culprit. Call her the cookie monster.

It's time to muster up willpower before Keri focuses on a lifestyle change. She felt healthier when those pounds melted off her medium frame. Somehow though, the pounds conjured up a foolproof system for finding their way back to her like bloodhounds following a scent. Keri's weight should be unrelated to how she is perceived by others. Even so, she allows those digits to regulate her self-esteem. Why can't she appreciate the beautiful woman in her reflection that others see? *When will these intrusive thoughts stop harassing me?*

Beauty comes in all shapes and sizes. Keri knows her comfort zone; she is familiar with the intense clutch of discomfort. Stepping into jeans that feel stitched on is a prime example. Reluctant to exhale is another leading example. She longs to feel content living in her skin. It's time for a diversion and the obsession with the scale must end. *Maybe I'll chuck it out the window!*

But Keri's goal is not to show off a thin body because thin doesn't necessarily measure up to good health. Magazine covers and social media posts underscore that model thin is what every girl or woman should replicate. Keri doesn't read those magazines or focus on the models. Society isn't her enemy; self-deprecation is her enemy.

With friends, family, a loving husband, and two adorable children, Keri isn't alone in the world. All is right in the universe when her kids wrap their little arms around her. All is right in the universe when her husband pulls her into an embrace and whispers, "Honey, you are the best thing that came into my life."

She is loved. She is enough. So, when will she offer the same compassion to herself?

"Baby steps," Keri says for the beige walls to hear.

"They're just numbers. I won't fall for their lies."

***

## Author Commentary

Keri's narrative is fiction, but I can insert it into my life story for an accurate fit. When hurtful words are tossed at us, they remain audible. We cannot throw them back because their effect is branded in our psyche. Traumatic moments and events stick with us regardless of how vigorously we try to peel them away from our memory. I endured similar moments on the school playground as a chubby little girl. Throughout the years, I could gain ten to twenty pounds, then lose it, stare at my reflection, and still view myself as chubby. I dislike the word fat, so I never use it. No one deserves to be called fat.

My worst critic is myself, but the criticism has softened. Caring about what others think is no longer significant. I still consider myself an emotional eater because I choose food for comfort or celebration. I don't reach for the bottle, light a cigarette, or pop a pill. However, I've learned to manage the cravings to maintain a healthy weight. That shiny scale still lures me but only periodically. If my clothes begin to hug uncomfortably, I know what to do. And I won't starve myself.

As my 100-year-old father-in-law says, "Everything is fine in moderation." I don't want to live without bread or an occasional cookie or piece of cake. And let us not forget chocolate! The amalgamation of fun into our busy lives is essential to balance setbacks. Indulging in the foods I love is part of that fun framework. But I can regulate the indulgences because who is in control? I am!

My husband and I love each other deeply, still after sharing thirty-five years. It saddens him when I get down on myself. He loves me for my heart, soul, and beauty, inside and out (his words). Our daughter and son are adults now, and while they witnessed moments when I was upset about extra pounds, I never wanted this issue to affect them. Fortunately, my obsession with the scale and weight never became their obsession, although I know it wasn't easy for them to see their mom hurting.

Ten to twenty pounds may not seem like a lot to lose. I can't speak for anyone except myself. So regardless of the number, shedding the pounds requires willpower and a modified lifestyle to sustain weight loss success. It takes an enormous amount of effort. I have experienced highs and lows on this growth journey to obtain the body positivity I deserve and to see myself as others see me. I slip infrequently, but I have gradually cultivated compassion for myself.

Many people struggle with body insecurities, so I hope my story will serve as inspiration and consolation. If you are one of these individuals, soak up my honesty and vulnerability. Embrace the reassurance that treating yourself with kindness is pivotal.

I have never been transparent about this issue which has caused me emotional turmoil for half a century. Only to my family and close friends have I exposed this weakness (my word choice). I admit that sharing my narrative feels liberating.

To summarize, we are all humans dealing with a concern that causes pain or anxiety. However, we are not oblivious that loving ourselves is imperative as well as ongoing. After all, no one climbs Mount Everest overnight! **Love the person you are because when we ultimately offer compassion to ourselves, we can fully love others, eternally.**

© Lauren Scott 2023

*A privilege...*

# CHAPTER TEN
## GRATEFUL & GRACEFUL GRANDPARENTING
## BY MIRIAM HURDLE

### Grateful and Graceful of Grandparenting

In most situations, a person can choose to be or not to be a parent. When our children decide to be parents, it's not up to us to play a role as a grandparent in our grandchildren's lives. Being a grandparent is not a right, it's a privilege.

I had been living in Southern California since 1980. My only daughter, Mercy, went to the University of Portland in Oregon, graduated in 2007, and got married in 2011. The chances of having her move back to California were slim. In fact, I was happy for her to stay in Portland for many reasons. Mercy and her husband, Will, love outdoor activities. Portland offers them the adventures of camping, hiking, skiing, rafting, and all kinds of water sports. I retired in 2011. It made sense for me to travel to visit them as often as I could. The advantage of frequent flying was earning mileage for free tickets for more travel.

Mercy was born the day after Christmas. She sometimes had her birthday parties with friends the week before or after Christmas, but I always tried to have a birthday dinner with her on her birthday. In 2016, Lynton and I visited Mercy and Will in Portland. We had Christmas dinner at her house, but we took them to a restaurant to celebrate her birthday.

In early January 2017, just three weeks after we saw them, I wanted to visit them again. I got on the phone with Mercy to let her know we wanted to see them in March. She seemed to be super excited about our next visit. During our phone conversations in the following weeks, she told me she was doing some decluttering. The organization seems to be in our genes. Mercy and I find satisfaction and delight in decluttering. Yet this time around, when I heard she was decluttering, a little bird told me something else was going on.
"Mercy, are you pregnant?"

She tried to distract my attention by talking about something else. I went along with the conversation.
In the meantime, I had the urge to tell my husband, but I tried very hard to hold this urge. A week went by, and I couldn't hold it any longer.

"I think Mercy is pregnant!" I finally broke the silence. One week before our trip to Portland, Mercy called and suggested we Skyped each other. During Skype time, Mercy and Will revealed Mercy's pregnancy. They showed us the ultrasound films. We learned that her due date was September 19. She said she was going to wait and tell us in person, but she couldn't even wait for one more week. She wanted to tell us, but the phone call was not enough. She wanted us to see the ultrasound. Hence, the Skype. We talked for a long time, then gave each other a virtual group hug before saying goodbye.

Mercy and Will could easily find out whether they were having a boy or a girl, yet they decided not to know. They wanted to do it the old fashion way or keep it as a surprise. The baby's bedroom was not painted in pink or blue. It was a neutral color.

Mercy's Baby Shower was on Saturday, August 19. Her best friend hosted the shower. I was invited to be on the hosting team. There were several creative activities, such as filling out a "Guessing" card to guess the baby's gender, weight, height, and eye color. Another activity was filling out an "I Wish" card addressing to the baby the thing they wish the baby will be or will do. As part of the support, the hostess had the ladies sign up for a "Meal Train" to bring meals to Mercy and Will after the baby was born.

Mercy wanted to work as long as she could so she could take longer maternity leave to care for the baby. It sounded like a good plan.

I was retired from my school administration job, but I had an after-school tutoring business that required my presence. For that reason, I had planned on traveling back and forth between helping Mercy and attending my business. My plan was to arrive in Portland five days before the baby was born and stayed for ten days. Then I would spend several days in California and several weeks in Portland, alternatively, for the following months to help the new parents.

I arrived on Thursday, September 14. Mercy started taking time off from work on Monday. She had a check-up at the doctor's office the day before I got there.
"The baby will be late, Mom."
"What did the doctor say?"
"She said the baby's position is good. I can wait. If the baby is not ready to come out by the 40th week, she can perform an induced labor."
"How do you feel?"
"I feel good and feel energetic."
"Let me know what you want me to do."
"Sure, I'll think about that and let you know."

Ten days had gone by, and the baby was not ready to meet the world yet. It was time for me to return to California. I was reluctant to leave because the baby could come out anytime by now.

"I'll keep my phone by my side all the time. Have Will call me as soon as you're on the way to the hospital."
"We'll do that, Mom."

My next trip going back to Portland was on Wednesday, September 27, only four days away. Lynton was going with me. I turned up the ringtone on my phone. I glanced at it constantly in case Will texted me.

I repacked my bag and added more things to it because I would stay for four weeks on my next trip. Mercy called me on Tuesday evening.

"Mom, the baby is almost ready to come out to meet with us. I went to the doctor today because I started having contractions and was dilated to 4 centimeters."

"Wow, how exciting! I'm so happy for you. We'll see you in the morning. If you're in the hospital already, we'll go straight from the airport."

"Thanks, Mom. We'll call you."

Mercy had been excited and celebrated the process of pregnancy by capturing the moments in photos. She posed by a tall chalkboard to chronicle her weekly weight gain and the look of her belly! What an overwhelming joy of parenthood, and the amazing wonder of bringing a new life into this world. The family and community were extremely enthusiastic and supportive. This gave them firm assurance and confidence.

We arrived on September 27 at 1:50 pm. When I turned off the airplane mode of my phone, there was a text message from Will letting us know Mercy was in labor. We took a taxi straight from the airport to the hospital. We stayed with Mercy until 7:00 pm. Mercy's dilation was progressing steadily, but the baby wasn't ready to arrive yet. Will asked us to take his car to go back to their house and wait for him to call us.

I went to bed with the phone next to me and was ready to head out the door as soon as Will called us for any news. I couldn't sleep but tried to rest. The phone rang at 4:00 am.

"Mercy had the baby. She didn't want me to call you earlier because she was in pain. She was not ready to have you around to see her in pain."

"How is Mercy now? Is it a boy or girl?"

"It's a girl. Mercy feels better now."

"Okay. We're on our way. Tell us some more when we get there."

"Okay. See you."

I wish they had called me when Mercy went into the delivery room. I was hoping to support her by being there, even if I were in the waiting room. I felt like something was missing. She didn't want me to see her when she was in pain. Did she cry? Did she scream? She might have felt crying was a sign of weakness. During my cancer treatment in 2009, she said my strength was her example. Did I show her only my strengths, but not my weaknesses? Did I tell her I cried to sleep? I should have told her, so she felt okay to let me know she suffered. Well, I respected her decision.

It was dark at 4:00 am. I was glad we went to the hospital earlier. On our way back to Mercy's house, we tried to remember the directions. We didn't use Google Maps in 2017. We arrived at the hospital and went straight to Mercy's room. The baby was in the same room with her. The nurse was changing her diaper. The setup in the maternity ward differed from the days when I gave birth to Mercy. During those days, they put all the babies together in a separate room. Relatives could only see the babies through the window. I liked the new setup of having the babies in the same rooms as the mothers. What a great idea to let the mothers see the babies all the time, hold them, and feed them right there in the same rooms.

After we washed our hands, the nurse handed the baby to us. It was surreal to hold the baby in my arms. The baby was in Mercy's womb yesterday. She was in my arms at this moment. My heart was full. I held the baby briefly, then handed her over to Lynton.

"How are you, Mercy?"

"Tired."

"She was in the delivery room for a long time," Will said.

"Was it a smooth delivery?" I wanted to know more.

"The dilation went from 4 centimeters to 9 centimeters but stopped there. Then it went back to 8. It went up and down for a while." Mercy recalled what the doctor said.

"Mercy was in great pain. At first, she didn't want to have the epidural anesthesia injection, but the pain was too much to bear, so she agreed to take the injection." Will described the intensity of the moments.

"I wish to have been here for you, Mercy." I rubbed her arm.

"The doctor said the baby was in distress. She wanted to perform a Cesarean Section (C-section). We agreed. It turned out that the umbilical cord wrapped around the baby's neck twice. Mercy pushed hard. The baby tried to come out, but the umbilical cord held her back. The C-section saved the struggles from Mercy and the baby." Will added.

Oh, what a relief! The C-section was done in time to

prevent any harm to the baby. Thank you, God.

"Mercy, you're tired from the pushing. Your belly will feel sore from the C-section when the anesthesia is worn off. I had a C-section for your birth."

"I know, Mom."

"Close your eyes to get some rest. We'll be here for a while."

"Okay."

We asked the nurse to take a picture of us with the baby in my arms. The nurse instructed us to record the feeding, the bay's pees, and the poops on the whiteboard. The doctor would discharge Mercy and the baby when the baby had a steady routine.

The feeding time was a challenge. Mercy tried different positions of holding the baby so that the baby could latch to her nipples easier. She didn't have the back strength to move her body because of the C-section pain in her lower belly. She could only use her arms to adjust to the position of the baby. Will tried to help. The nurse tried to help.

Mercy looks frustrated. I better not say anything. I don't want to cause additional anxiety for her. She'll figure it out. All mothers do.

The nurse was wonderful. She said different positions worked for different moms and babies. She showed holding the baby like holding a baseball under the arm. She asked Mercy to bend her wrist into the baby so that her arm maintain the grip of the baby close to her. She helped Mercy to hold the baby's head to stabilize the baby's mouth to latch to her nipple.

Mercy tried it. The nurse brought some pillows over and asked Mercy to rest her elbow on the pillow. Will was on the side to support the baby's body while Mercy moved the baby's mouth toward the nipple. It looked good. The baby sucked well. We all cheered for the success. Lynton and I stayed in the hospital most of the day for several days. We took breaks to eat in the cafeteria so that Will can be alone with Mercy. I know. The nurse was there often. I helped to change the baby's diaper. I also helped to keep records on the whiteboard. The lower half of the 4'x8' whiteboard was getting full.

"Have you chosen a name for baby Rossi yet?" I asked them both.
"No, but we will soon," Will said.
"Take your time. The nurse just needs to put the baby's name on the paper on the day of discharge."
"I know, Mom. We'll have it by then."

I didn't know until much later that they had a list of names ready. They wanted the baby to feel good about her name by calling her those names. Eventually, the baby had a favorite response to the name "Autumn" and that was how they named the baby "Autumn."

It was time for the proud parents and baby Autumn to go home. When we arrived home, to our great surprise, their friends decorated their front door with balloons and a welcome message. I was happy to capture their homecoming moment.

Autumn's bedroom was set up with a crib, a dresser, and a changing pad on top. Mercy wanted to use a bassinet to keep baby Autumn in their room for a few months. It would be easier for her to feed Autumn at night.

The nurse helped to take care of Autumn at night. They now had to get up to feed her and change her. Will and I didn't want Mercy to do it all by herself. Besides, she wouldn't be able to move too fast for a while until the scar from the C-section healed. After discussing the options, we decided to put Autumn in the middle of the living room, and we all slept on the couches. Mercy would feed Autumn every 2 to 3 hours, but Will and I helped to change her diaper.

I guess nobody got too much sleep except the baby for the first night. The next day, Mercy said I could sleep in my room and she and Will could take care of the baby at night in their room.

For the following four weeks, I helped to cook, do the laundry, and do other household chores so that they could focus on being new parents. Will took his paternity leave and used some of his vacation time to stay home. They stayed in their room talking about different things. I usually kept busy doing this and that. Unless they volunteered to, otherwise, I took it as part of their learning to be parents. They might want to try this way and that way before settling on a routine.

Baby Autumn continued having a problem latching on to Mercy's nipples. During the one-month checkup, Mercy shared with the pediatrician about the situation. It turned out that the baby had a tongue tie. The pediatrician performed a procedure for baby Autumn by making a small cut to the tissue connecting the tongue to the floor of the mouth (lingual frenulum) allowing her tongue to move more freely to latch her mom's nipples when sucking. The procedure was successful and helpful. It was a great relief for Mercy's feeding anxiety.

Mercy and Will were active in sports. They did a triathlon together. They did the cross-country skiing and climbed to the top of Mt. Adams. Mercy was in good shape before the C-section. The nurse asked Mercy to walk around the hospital floor within 24 hours of the delivery and she walked every day.

Mercy felt strong and could move freely after two weeks. She sometimes used a baby wrap carrier to carry baby Autumn on her chest to go for a walk. Halloween was around the corner. I would go with her on walks and take photos of the Halloween decorations in the neighborhood.

After Autumn was born, Lynton stayed for several days before returning to California. I stayed until the end of October. Other than doing the household chores, I took care of Autumn when Mercy and Will went out to run errands. When baby Autumn was asleep, she often had a startle reflex when her back jerked lightly. I liked to let her nap on my chest. When she jerked, I put my hands on her back to calm her. She only had the startle reflex for a few months.

Two months after she was born, Autumn flew with her

parents to Southern California to meet her extended family. Will went back to work already after his paternity leave. Mercy was still on leave. They spent four days with us. On Thanksgiving Day, we had dinner with Lynton's family. My sister and her family also joined us. My husband was the first one in his family to become a grandpa. It was quite exciting. People were eager to hold the beautiful baby.

When we went to visit my daughter and her family for Christmas that year, Portland welcomed us with a blanket of snow at the airport on the day of Christmas Eve. It was our first white Christmas. Portland rarely got snow.

As soon as we arrived at Mercy's house, we wanted to have some photos taken before the snow was gone.

It looked like Autumn had gained several pounds and was a couple of inches taller since she was born. Will told us she liked to be held facing forward so that she could look around. Family, friends, and strangers alike fell in love with her large blue eyes right away when they met her and saw her pictures.

Mercy had a Baby Play Gym in the living room for her to play when she was awake. She loved to follow the mirror in her Baby Play Gym. We went to see the Christmas lights on Christmas Eve, had dinner at home and opened presents on Christmas Day, and played card games after dinner. Will held her on his lap when we played the game. Autumn's eyes focused on the cards as if she could read them.

From September 2017 to December 2018, after the initial stay of a month, I went to Portland once a month and stayed for five days. The idea of moving close to Mercy and my granddaughter appeared in my mind constantly. I secretly prayed and waited for the right timing.

In June 2019, I babysat Autumn by myself while Mercy and Will went to Iceland on vacation. Some friends said I was brave. Some said it would make me tired, but I could handle it. The advice was, "When she sleeps, you sleep."

Mercy made a spreadsheet of suggested daily schedules and activities, a list of her friends and phone numbers, and the doctor and phone number. At first, I felt strange, as if she thought I didn't know how to take care of a baby. Yet I appreciated her thoroughness. My mind was at ease without worrying about what to do to fill the days. They rented a car for me even though I wasn't planning on driving it too much.

They took a late afternoon flight and arrived early the next day to make the most of their trip. Before boarding, Mercy texted me, "I missed Autumn already. Please send a lot of pictures." "I will do that." I returned her text.

When Autumn woke up in the morning, she looked for Mommy and Daddy. I said, "Mommy will be back. Daddy will be back." She said, "Daddy went to work. Mommy went to work. Daddy will be back. Mommy will be back."

We went to the park in the afternoon. There were kids playing with the water feature. I looked at the backpack. There was a change of clothes, so I let Autumn play with the other kids. She ran through the squirting and swaying water, giggling.

The next day, before nap time, Autumn had a temperature of 101.2° F. After she woke up from the nap, the temperature went up to 103° F. I kept Mercy updated. Deep down, I regretted letting Autumn play with the water for too long on the previous day. I hoped her temperature wouldn't prolong. Most of all, I didn't want Mercy to cut their vacation short.

I called Mercy's friends to pick up a few items from the store for me. I also told them Autumn had a temperature. They came after their work. One of them was a nurse. She checked Autumn's temperature and wrote some instructions for me. The other friend bought what I needed, plus some Popsicles.

Autumn had a good night's sleep. I put her on a soft diet, plus the Popsicle. We didn't go to the park. And just did some quiet activities around the house. By the afternoon, her temperature came back to normal. It was such a tremendous relief for me. My first-time babysitting Autumn all by myself turned out okay. I'm glad Mercy didn't have to cut their vacation short. We exchanged messages and photos several times a day.

"It seems to be a 24-hour thing." Mercy messaged me. "I think so. I'm glad it was a 24-hour thing." I returned her message and attached some photos of Autumn eating a Popsicle.

On the remaining days, we went to the park and the

library and walked around the neighborhood. On the day of their return, Mercy and Will arrived home in the late evening. Autumn was in bed already, but she was excited to see Mommy and Daddy when she woke up the next day.

Being an educator, watching her grow and learn unique skills was an amazement. I loved to keep track of her developmental progress. I paid more attention to her reading development. My daughter Mercy and Will started reading bedtime stories to her as soon as Autumn came home from the hospital. They wanted to establish her habit of reading. The cloth books or board books were part of her toys. Before she turned two, she seemed to prefer books rather than manipulative toys. Mercy had age-appropriate toys for her, but she picked up books to flip the pages more often than to press the buttons for the toys. Her favorite books when she was around one year old were a set of 2"x2" ten nursery rhyme books. They were the right size for her small hands. She picked out the books one at a time, brought them to us, turned around, and sat on our laps. We sang nursery rhymes to her as we flipped the pages.

Autumn kept up her interest in books. By three years old, she had a long attention span to listen to books with over 1,000 words. Even though she didn't understand the meaning of all sentences, she picked up simple meanings and words she could relate with. When we repeated reading the same book, she would interact by saying the names of the characters or actions corresponding to the illustrations. As we repeated reading the same book again and again, she remembered more details.

The thematic books she enjoyed and found funny were the Magic School Bus books. She flipped through the Magic School Bus book on dinosaurs. She could name all the dinosaurs. The book made learning fun by inventing funny names with illustrations. One picture had a sock as the head and a body of a dinosaur and was named Sockasaurus. Another picture has a banana head and was named Bananasaurus. We made it fun by inventing our own, such as naming the fingers Fingerasaurus.

Mercy took her to the library to check out books. They checked out as many books as the library tote bag could hold. It was about twenty-five books. We read at least half of them as soon as we came home. When we went somewhere in the car, she wanted to have an entire bag of books available to read. One time when she was around three years old before we used book bags, she insisted on bringing many books to the car. We tried to tell her to bring just a few, but she picked out a stack of about ten large-size books and carried them, walking from the house to the car on her little feet. Well, how can we discourage her from the love of books?

For a short while, I worried that she only read books but did not keep a balance between books and other activities and social skills. But my worries soon puffed away. I watched her playing well with friends. She enjoyed hiking, rock climbing, biking, camping, swimming, and other adventurous family activities.

I saved boxes of books from my teaching days. I went through the books and took the vocabulary-appropriate books to her on my visits to her. She knew I had something for her every time. She would ask, "What is in your bag, Grandma?" I would take out the books and say, "These books are yours."

I visited my daughter Mercy at the end of February 2020. Her friend planned a baby shower on Saturday for her second baby. I arrived on Thursday. Her friend called on Friday to cancel the shower because she was exposed to someone who might have been exposed to the Coronavirus. She didn't want to risk any harm to my daughter's pregnancy.

Will took Autumn out for a bike ride. Mercy and I talked about things while I gave her a head and shoulder massage. She had a good night's sleep and felt better the next morning. She was relieved that it wasn't a Coronavirus.

We took Autumn to the Children's Museum on Saturday. Autumn went to one play area with a baby room. She practiced taking off and putting on the clothes for the baby doll. Autumn had a baby doll at home to practice putting on the diaper and feeding the doll. She also had books on having a baby sister or being a big sister. It was a wonderful way to prepare her to welcome a little sister into her family.

As soon as I came home to Southern California, I booked the next trip on March 24, four days before Mercy's due day. They needed someone to watch my two-and-a-half-year-old granddaughter, Autumn.

On Thursday, March 11, The California Governor announced the social distancing policy. On March 17, Mercy and I had a video chat. She said she was worried about my health and didn't want me to get sick from the travel. I tried to ease her worry and still wanted to go. After talking for a few minutes, I realized she was worried that if I got sick, it would affect the baby. I then told her I would cancel my trip.

On Sunday, March 22, Mercy went to the hospital at 5:00 am with a 7cm dilation. She video-called me at 9:00 am before taking a nap. Baby Nora was born at 12:30 pm weighed 6 pounds and 7 ounces. Will sent me a couple of photos of baby Nora. Mercy video called me again around 1:30 pm when she was back in her room. The doctor discharged her on Tuesday afternoon, even though the baby didn't eat too much and didn't have too many pees and poops yet. The doctor sent her home with distant support because she would be safer at home. She called me again on Wednesday when she was feeding the baby. They were thrilled to have Nora.

I later found out that on March 22, they left Autumn at home while she was sleeping. Will dropped off Mercy at the hospital and rushed back home. Will was not with Mercy when baby Nora was born. In the afternoon, their friends watched Autumn for a couple of hours so that Will could go see Mercy and the new baby. How I wish to have been there at these memorable moments!

COVID-19 was such an unusual time for births, birthdays, weddings, funerals, or being ill in the hospital.

Families could not be with their loved ones during these memorable and critical moments.

We didn't go to Autumn's birthday party in September this year. Mercy sent us photos of the new party style. They set up a long table in the front yard in front of the door with individually wrapped food items. There were chairs set up six feet apart. Only a dozen people were invited. Everyone wore a face mask. Neighbors who drove by would press the honk slightly to cheer the birthday girl.

Six months after Nora's birth, we traveled to Portland to meet Nora for the first time. My daughter Mercy and I planned carefully. They self-quarantined for two weeks prior to our visit. We did the same. I booked the plane tickets in the Main cabin with premium seats. The idea was not to pass through so many passengers on the plane to get to our seats. We wore face masks on the plane all the time unless when eating or drinking. No coffee was served except canned drinks and individually wrapped snacks.

Our five-day visit to the grandkids was precious. We had fun doing things even though it was limited by the Covid. We went to a pumpkin farm. Mercy carried Nora in her baby carrier. Autumn visited the cows, goats, and pigs. She and Daddy went on a hayride, train ride, and jumped on a giant bouncing bed. Other than the pumpkin farm visit, we stayed home most of the time. Nora was in her Sit-to-Stand Activity Center, spinning around and playing with the toys. Autumn tried to interact with her by making her bounce up and down, except she didn't know how hard or soft to bounce her.

Autumn was excited to see us. She came into our room to wake us up every morning and cuddled with us. If she didn't see Lynton, she asked, "Where is Grandpa?" "I think he went to get a newspaper," I said. She wanted Lynton to read the newspaper to her. Autumn's language development amazed me. Sometimes when the grownups carried on a conversation at the dinner table, she would ask, "What are you talking about?" She wanted to be part of the conversation. As for the grownups, we played board games three nights in a row.

Nora and Autumn were perfect reading buddies. They often read side by side. She not only looked at the illustrations but pointed at the words and moved her fingers along the lines. She loved drawing and coloring. Amazingly, she colored within the lines better than many of my kindergarten students. She became quite a chatter box speaking in long sentences. They had a family night decorating gingerbread cookie for Christmas in 2022.

During the activity, Mercy said, "May I borrow the pink when you're done using it?" When the not-quite-three-year-old Nora needed purple or other frosting colors, she would say, "May I borrow the purple when you're done using it?" We looked at each other and smiled.

The year 2022 was a major turning point in our life. We visited the grandkids in the middle of August. Then we rented a car to drive to Port Angeles, Washington. Mercy took us to the car rental because Will was at work. I sat in the middle of the backseat between the girls. Autumn held my hand all the way from their home to the car rental. When we said goodbye to the girls, Autumn was sad, broke out, and cried terribly. We lingered a while to calm her down and promised to come back to see her. She said, "But it's going to be a long time."

We reluctantly left her to go on our journey. During our trip to Port Angeles, Lynton expressed an interest in moving to Portland to be close to the grandkids. I had been waiting for this moment for five years. His entire family is in Southern California. I didn't want to take him away from his family. But there was a big change during these five years. Some of his siblings' children are married with children. They're busy with their own satellite families. I think the critical point was when his mom passed away in the previous month. For years, he felt obligated to stay in California to be close to his mom. Ever since his mom moved to the memory care home, the extended family didn't get together as often. I think his mom's passing released an obligation to stay in California. The grandkids are getting close to him, and he finds more interest and meaning to be close to them.

For the following four months, we actively searched for a new home in Portland. We hoped to find a place within a 20-minute drive of Mercy's home. In the meantime, we connected with an agent to list our Southern California home. We took three months to pack and stored our belongings in public storage. We got two offers twelve days after we listed our house on the market. On December 7, the day of closing the escrow, we drove one car to Portland. Lynton wanted to rent a truck to move our belongings instead of hiring someone from a moving company. Driving to Portland would give him an idea of the road condition.

We stayed with Mercy for one month while searching for a new home. I did a lot of homework before our arrival. We spent several days visiting homes with our agents. Lynton fell in love with one house. We made an offer right away. After a few days of negotiation, the owners accepted our offer, and the escrow was closed in less than 30 days.

We've been living in our new home since the beginning of January 2023. We got together on special occasions, such as Nora's birthday in March, Easter in April, and Mother's Day in May. We helped to watch the girls when Mercy and Will went on a short vacation or a night out in the evenings. We watched the girls when they attended social or work functions. Both Autumn and Nora are taking lessons in gymnastics, ballet, swimming, and ice skating. Autumn is taking piano lessons. I helped to pick up the girls from their preschool and take them to different classes.

It has been a blessing to Lynton and I to have the grandkids in our lives. They've put joy in our hearts and smiles on our faces. They've made us feel energetic and enthusiastic. They've brought out the best in us. We always looked forward to spending time with them. Life is enjoyable for our family because we live close to each other and are there for each other.

© Miriam Hurdle 2023

*Silver linings.*

# CHAPTER ELEVEN
## SEEING THROUGH
## BY YVETTE PRIOR

At the time of putting this book together, my husband and I were in the process of moving. We never expected the challenges that would come with a poor fit with the realtor we chose to sell our house. She was a nice person and we saw many of her strengths but she was inexperienced and had a completely different approach to selling a house. In addition, there was an unneeded rushed timeline and we learned lessons about how hurry and pressure are a bad mix when it comes to making choices. The miserable experience came with many silver linings and my spouse and I bonded as we coped. In some ways, it reminded us of the coping we did while managing exhausting (and expensive) visitation litigation with my husband's ex-wife in the 1990s.

Now when I say the term, *realtor stress*, each person will instantly apply their meaning to try and understand what I might mean. I mentioned that we had realtor stress to one lady and she reminded me to make sure that we remembered to *compromise*, which indicated her take on the topic was that folks often failed to compromise. *Sigh.* I did smile at how quickly her first thought was that we might not be compromising. That was not the case for us – even though at one point it might have seemed that way; instead, we had poor counsel and a realtor who did not seem to understand the market and seemed to be overly concerned about what the buyer's agent wanted (as if they were partnered).

The realtor that we chose had good intentions and I am sure there are more details to her story that we do not know. She also had someone whispering in her ear with specific advice (still training?) and so she likely had plenty of her own stress to work through and learn from. We do empathize with her; however, we realized that her inexperience was a huge factor. We had to get outside counsel, from a few sources, which became part of the silver linings, especially when we met Laneisha - a local realtor with 20+ years of experience in our area. We also found a special new home to buy during this rushed and pressure-filled process, which made it easier to yield rather than change realtors or go to mediation.

You would have to walk in our shoes to fully understand the pressure we felt. The two other times we sold a house it unfolded seamlessly with nothing to write about. However, this current experience felt like moving through a storm. To share part of my story, I decided to share entries I wrote in my journal during the time of selling, moving, and starting life in our new home.

## 1. Growth

How do you know – when you grow?
Are things more obvious when we don't grow or if we
feel stuck? In a rut?
How do you see personal growth – the kind that is subtle,
hidden, remote?
We know maturity comes by moving through trials.
Resilience is built.

How do you know – when you grow?
Is it with an expanded outlook?
Seeing through a clear window as opposed to a limiting
mirror that only sees what we want to see?
Do we identify growth when we understand, sympathize,
and empathize better?

- Growth manifests with humbleness.
- Growth shows when we can see more about how
  others experience a situation.
- Growth means we heal. Recover. Repair.
  Replenish.
- Growth means we have concern for others and
  serve. Giving is, indeed, the highest form of living.
- Growth also means we tend to our life and needs.

Take heed...
We also need to think of our path.
Our work.
We are not being a jerk when we take care of what God
has called us to do. What we need to do.
We need to examine each situation.

Create space. Think of others.
Love and grace.
Also comes from taking care of our space.

How do you know – when you grow?
Could it be seen with inner peace and contentment during
the storm?
Is growth seen through bringing a more positive you into
the world? One that does not bulldoze and clobber others
with demandingness. Is growth about having a softer
approach to others – even when stressed?

Growth is not about perfection
Growth shows when we mature from mistakes.
 Cope with challenges.
 Learn as we go.
Yes, this is how we grow.
Grit develops. It does not just appear or show.

## 2. More Than Fine

There's a rhythm in the world
 a certain clock
 varies dock to dock
 sometimes smooth
 other times a swirl

The rhythm here
brings cheer
this new home of ours
comes with twinkling stars
 birds in the morning
 butterflies in the afternoon

Cicada's at dusk
fireflies with the moon

Do we appreciate the many silver linings?
Sure do.
We are more than fine.

Overlap, interplay
togetherness and sway
we are all connected
sharing the sun's rays

My favorite tea, smells differently
the water here, has a different flair
I savor the flavor, sip slowly
becoming refined
one day at a time

Do we know to be present in the moment?
Sure do.
We are more than fine.

Feeling humble, lowly
yet also elevated
filled with gratefulness
overwhelmed by God's goodness

The sun emerges
bringing light my way
It is actually the world turning
as I start a new day

Moved 1,000 miles

new time zone
new garden zone
new life zone
how do people define home?

Do we miss the east coast?
Sure do.
Yet, we are more than fine.

Four weeks of settling in
ready for the NEW
ready for the NOW
    still adjusting
    but our *third act* has begun
    feels right, becoming fun

Do we miss what we had in the past?
Sure do.
Yet, we are more than fine.

What is meant to last? What do we really own and for
how long?
Fortunes and materials come with a fleeting song
Everyone has a life cycle
    so do life's highs and lows
    so do material items
All part of human growth
as seasons, and other changes, come and go

How do we handle loss
    stress
    dross
    setback

> lack
> attacks
> change
> feeling wronged
> feeling hurt?
It comes down to sometimes tasting dirt
God exalts the humble
> wait, trust, grow
> develop patience

Do we have a heaven bias?
Sure do.
We are more than fine.

Heaven anchors our worldview.
There's a rhythm in our life
that moves to the beat of faith, which is kinda great
melody of God's light and love
fills us, covers us
We bank on heaven as our true home
> loss can be gain.
> less can be more.
> more can be less.
> more can be more.
Times of loss and times of more.
We try not to keep score.
An open hand rather than a closed fist.
More about what is, less about what if?

Do we know things could be worse?
Sure do.
We are more than fine.

A new house is like a foreign country
At first it feels like living in outer space.
So we keep a steady pace
    set up and nestle down
    embracing this new town
Seeing through - as God led us here
new dock, new pier
       lessons in letting go
       time for a new show.

Do we know that we have great things coming?
Sure do.
We are more than fine.

## 3. We Endured

"Sign us up," we said
nodding our head
as we agreed
to let her lead
trusting her with the house sale
    unaware of the gale
    the tailspin
    that would come our way
Having a novice lead
    with completely different views
challenged us through and through
    yet we stand
    we endured
to now enjoy today

We had no idea that so much dismay
would come our way...

the rushing and misunderstandings
sense of pressure and urgency
making decisions because of momentum
maybe not quite under duress
    but if you really felt our stress
    you would have a sense of the mess
as to how someone makes confused decisions
    that could not be undone
baffled moments
wondering how we ended up there
pondering what to do
    go to mediation
    or push through?
A lack of trust while being rushed
is messed up!

- Learned what it is like to freeze from pressure. We already experienced fight or flight.
- One time it felt like we said, "No" 55 times.
- We also learned that persuasive wording can get you to make decisions that later did not feel right.
- As a researcher, I better understood why we give participants at least 48 hours to process consent.
- I also better understood the 72-hour window of "changing your mind" that is offered after some large purchases.

When things move fast
my husband and I tend to acquiesce to tasks
    part of being decision-makers
    part of trusting those who lead
Yet it still baffles, the more we see
    how the unneeded rushing

fueled misery

I finally watched some documentaries
 while still setting up our new house
Healing came my way in trickles
 as each story rippled
 into my story
 about seeing through
 rebuilding after stressful things
Reminders that those with a grateful heart sing

We count so many blessings
My husband often goes through the list
 so many gifts
 so many things to be grateful for
 like Laneisha Winston coming our way
 to empower and infuse the day
  she brought support and advice
  divine appointment, oh so nice

We endured, on course we stayed
to now enjoy today.

## 4. Ending Strong

God does exalt the humble.
Gives grace to the down and out.

If we did not find Eulea's house
 life would be different right now
 not sure exactly how
 but we like the way things turned out

We likely would've had lawyers involved
    mediation to problem solve
    or we'd be moving months later
We still would have ended strong
Perhaps with more loss
not just in money – but other costs
    like more wear and tear to heal
    time with lawyers and mediation
    rather than closing a deal

God gives grace to those who need it.
    who ask for it.
    who wait on Him.
Grace is lavished on those who are parched and
wearing thin.
The day we found Eulea's house
    was at the height
    of what felt like a battle, a subtle fight

Everything took a turn
    when Chris was in the hall
        he found Eulea's yellow house
        we both stood tall
Fresh on the market
    led to an emergency trip
    that brought us away
    from the realtor vice grip

So many miscommunications
    so much *not* being said
    trying to piece things together
    what happened in realtor preview days?

Lack of trust is a big deal
    being too trusting at first
    led to confusion and stress
Yet that mess, led to where we are today.
    a place of strength and grace.


Sometimes the only way to reach the needed exit
    is to get on the highway and drive
The drive might come with stormy weather
    but your exit will arrive.
Our exit came while in a tailspin - trying to figure
    out what our realtor was doing
    and if she was still in training?


Confusion about us needing more time;
    she didn't seem to understand
Needing more time was not for preference – not for
comfort - sometimes it is a matter of logistics – and the
reality of needing more time was to get things done.
We failed to understand each other


House staging? *Sigh.*
Over-staging the house - as if dressing up her dolls
Over-staging to where it hid house features
    It felt slightly deceptive
    It felt highly not needed
      stressful
      not considerate of seller needs
      not considerate of what the situation needed
Not a good use of her time, either.
Not needed in a market where homes have multiple
offers on the first day (or they clamp an informal

partnership with a buyer during the preview days and staging is for the collection of brochures to add to files). The realtor circle is weird in some areas because "some" realtors do previews with other realtors and then they do not let you know what they all talked about.
Left guessing what went on behind the scenes.
    stressful
    wrong
not considerate of the seller's dignity
Busted trust!
But it all led to now singing
    a very sweet song
    as we talked our way along
    had prayer support
    to now end strong

God exalts the humble.
    gives grace to the forlorn
We went from torn and worn
    to now we soar
    ending strong
    is like a beautiful song

## 5. Now You Know

You've been schooled
not like a fool; instead, like a normal human
    who needed to learn
    turn by turn

Repeating mistakes
    is when foolishness creeps in
yet even then, there's grace

saving face
life is not a race
life is more than cold business decisions
sometimes we have less precision
so we embrace an ebb and flow
that might be needed as we go


Our story is less about the wrong realtor
more about the connections
more about the arrival of a new friend
*"You didn't know, what you didn't know"*
was the phrase Laneisha shared as she helped us see
through the stress
Her wise counsel and empowering words
girded us
finally felt understood


We wanted to be passive, and let our hired realtor do the
work but the increasing lack of trust
made us come across like jerks
We were dismayed
and constantly prayed
trusting God would lead
provide for every need


*Now we know what we didn't know*
and even though it was a messy show
After the storm, we look around
to see we landed on such beautiful ground
Many lessons learned
are held like a valuable gift
because experience
is what develops grit

Turn by turn, we humans learn
    we can, and *should*, learn more
    about what we don't know
        while not keeping score
        but improving
    making the most of today
    because things will be okay


Wouldn't it be great - to never make mistakes?
Well, we think it might be
    but mistakes help us see
    more about who we are
    how to improve
    how to cope and pull together
    adapting to up and down weather


I pondered the word *mistake*: error or faulty judgment
Just because something came with a storm, does it mean
it was a mistake?
If something doesn't work out, whether a job, a car, or a
realtor – does this mean we call it a mistake?
Perhaps not!


Even if we would make different choices if we could go
back – do some mistakes lead us to the proper path?
Bring us to the right exit ramp?
Do some mistakes help us carve the needed road?
Are errors, or mistakes, essential for human growth?
I think so!


*We don't know what we don't know...*
Laneisha Winston was right

and the way she girded us
brings me back to that Friday night
when we met a stranger who became a friend
    she offered support
    helped us to the end
While still staying within her legal bounds
she empowered us inside and out

I pondered the word *gird*: to fortify, strengthen, enliven
    She girded us through and through
    She said we shifted her energy –
        well, she shifted our energy too
A God appointment to meet her, this we know
    special encounters
    part of human growth
helping, giving, lending a hand
receiving, bonding, trusting
we need each other to endure and stand

Chris and I *now know what we didn't know* then
    We know what to do next time
    and that is why we have big smiles
    lessons learned
    will help us with the upcoming miles

## 6. What You Need

I stand a little taller today
The knot in my stomach
    feels looser, softer

The stress knot
    in my gut

untangles slow
I wish it could be cut
    but that is not always
    how we grow
    or heal from a stress rut

Restoration is often slow
    even after a rushed, flash sale of your house
    recovery needs time to be worked out

I wish healing was instant
    and that this was distant
    but we process lessons learned
    turn by turn

We decompress
    as the days go by
    variety in long conversation
      lots of small talks too
      processing this and that
    or shelfing the matter for breaks
      let it simmer and rest
      heal in the chest
    turn by turn
    we heal and learn

Good sleep and power naps
    as we unpack, settle in, debrief
So many silver linings, good grief
So much good to be seen.
Life is not always filled with such extremes
    but sometimes storms flood the scene
And those storms might just be

exactly what you need
    to proceed
    to succeed
    arrive and thrive
    to land
right where you need to be

## 7. Little Dots of Pink

Those little dots of pink
    that top my toes
    bring a smile
Just like pink Crepe Myrtle blooms do
    off in a distance
    warm hues
I sit back for a while
    soaking up the calm
    feeling the joy
    the new house becomes more familiar
    and the charm continues to dazzle
    I often forget about that realtor hassle

The many trees here are a desire of my heart
My book, *Avian Friends*, describes the start
of my appreciating trees, birds, and outdoors
and now, we are flooded with so much more

A hummingbird visits
    every afternoon
    I listen for its dull, hummin' tune
    as it lives outside the front room

While the splashes of subtle pinks

on this sunny July day
bring harmony my way
I shake my head in dismay
for the way God brought us here
as we gave Him every care

Pink is not my go-to color
    yet it was what I chose for nails
    a quick pedicure was significant
It marked a settling point in the move
    realtor stress no longer the groove

After many days of being up late
surviving the way our realtor chose to operate
15 days in the new place
with polished nails staring me in the face
all this nature surrounding
filling my heart, such a grounding

A small thing
    splashes of color
    with a beauty vibe
Yet a key part of nesting
    decompressing
    finding a new stride

## 8. Steak Bites

Steak bites satisfy
    juicy
    salty
    tender
    life-giving

The doggies look on
 poised
 begging posture
 waiting for any scraps
 juicy pieces will come their way
But first, I go to dine on the sweet patio
 where the pillars embrace me
 light orange pillows I see
 it enriches all the white
 as Eulea's garden brings delight
 such a sight
 to soak up
 while enjoying juicy steak bites

## 9. Six Weeks

Six weeks ago
we were in the net
of miscommunication
stress and upset
 baffled
 not grasping it

Six weeks ago, I was talking to a student
 who wanted to buy our house
 if the deal fell through
We were two days into the confusing contract
 the one we agreed to while feeling rushed
 pushed
 confused
The offers also felt *off*
 we felt trapped

not supported
it was really tough

We moved forward, confused
perplexity was thick
as our realtor was secretive
not forthcoming
we almost felt tricked

The secretive mode is the worse
Feeling *not in the know* is a horrible way to go
And if she raises her children with that approach
    she will raise little followers
    who stay small
But maybe she will change her approach
    as she also is now more *in the know*
    and she will continue to grow
    Why did she choose a secretive approach?
    we might not ever know

Now here we are, six weeks have passed
The storm truly did NOT last
Somehow it all worked out
Makes me want to shout:
    "Thank you, God, for all you do.
    Thank you, Jesus, for getting us through."

Sometimes six weeks
    can be a dull period of time
    slow-going seasons
    or just average-moving lines
Other times, six weeks can be intense
    like our recent experience

which did not make sense
Yet it became *green light go*
and now our third act unfolds
Six weeks led to much growth

## 10. At Home

Last sip of coffee
I finished looking at the map
    of the United States
Are we really living in this new state?
Yes, we are.
We feel quite at home
Partly because of this charming,
    mid-century abode
    the new job also brings a fresh work load
There are other things
    that connect with my heart
Small things
    we felt from the start
Feeling at home
    from variables I cannot describe
    essence
    sweet southern vibe
Walking the property, I feel so alive
I feel like I could be in Europe somewhere
or like this is "Anywhere, USA"
    How long will we stay?
    That is impossible to say.
In the meantime, we keep settling in
appreciating feeling at home again

## 11. Spilled Paint

Do you know how to clean up spilled paint? I do.
When a gallon tips over
    spills across the floor
    you go running out the door
    to get towels
    while knowing what is in store:
    cleaning up a huge mess!

Did you know that cleaning spilled paint is easier than it
looks? Quite a surprise.

- When a gallon of paint tips over, which has
  happened to me twice, it seems daunting and
  overwhelming. It seems like the floor might be
  forever stained and it will take hours to clean.
- One of the tips for cleaning spilled paint is to
  scoop and lift the paint with a putty knife or a long
  piece of cardboard.
- Some of the paint can also be saved that way.
  It depends on where the spill happened and if the
  paint became dirty.
- After the paint is scooped, the remaining paint
  wipes up easily.

    A recent paint spill was cleaned up in less than five
minutes. I marveled at how fast it went. The reason I
cleaned up the paint so easily, and with little stress, was
that I had previous experience. After the gray paint
spilled in the guest house, I was stopped in my tracks.
The cleaning detour was inconvenient and at first, I was
nervous the floor would be ruined. However, I quickly

remembered that I cleaned up spilled paint in our last house and knew it was not as bad as it looked.

This reminded me of problems in life. Sometimes when things come our way, it might seem more daunting and overwhelming than it really is. I also realized that the experience of moving through trials fortifies us and preps us for handling further trials.

- So many things in life might appear to be worse than they are. Are people this way too? I think so. Some people appear tougher and more abrasive than they are.
- We need to assess if we are viewing others with a cynical mirror and limiting bias or if we are trying to understand them through a window that considers alternative perspectives.

\*\*\*

I dedicated this book, on perspective taking, to my father-in-law, Paul, because he had so much perspective shaping and growth in his later years. We have often heard that you cannot teach an old dog new tricks, or that people might be too old to change, but this did not fully apply to Paul. It was slow going, but I still marvel at the small positive changes he made as his insight grew in his final six years on this earth. He did not get away from his addiction and needy, critical spirit; however, his self-awareness increased as he learned more about outlook, unhealthy responses, reframing, and small changes.

- I think everyone can improve outlook to understand others more and have better relationships.

- It might be difficult for some people to change, especially if they have well-established symptoms of a personality disorder or if they are set in their ways, but with effort and with the right approach, positive change can happen.

I do not look forward to cleaning up spilled paint. Hopefully, I will never have to clean it up again. However, if I do spill paint, I know to look beyond the immediate daunting mess. I know it looks worse than it is. I know that scooping the paint and then wiping the floor is easy to do and the final wipe-down brings so much satisfaction. Life's problems are often this way.

We fail forward by not getting overwhelmed; instead, we learn more about coping and find ways to enjoy life more.

© Yvette Prior 2023

*Tremendous patience.*

# CHAPTER TWELVE
## WINDING ROAD OF WRITING
## BY MABEL KWONG

Writing is something I love doing. I write all the time. Writing is a defining part of my identity, a natural way for me to express thoughts, emotions and what's important to me with the world. It was what I enthusiastically did for a living at one point. Writing and publishing a book is also one of my dreams.

The writing journey is often not a straight, smooth-sailing one with ups and downs along the way. When you're a writer, one moment you may imaginatively weave ideas into words with a passion. Other moments you may feel utterly dissatisfied with what you have written. Writing compelling stories brings me much joy. But there was a time when I wanted to quit writing altogether.

In this chapter, I share my experiences about understanding the challenges I faced on my writing journey. Through building mental resilience and toughness, I managed the difficulties of writing and worked towards maintaining wellness as a writer.

## My Writing Journey

Growing up in suburban Australia, reading and writing was an integral part of my essence. At school, I read every book on the shelf in kindergarten classes. I loved writing essays in English classes at school. Later at university, I loved writing even longer essays for my Arts Degree. For almost a decade I was a freelance non-fiction writer, writing about the concepts of multiculturalism and belonging. I published self-development pieces in magazines, books and online platforms while also hosting a globally engaged blog that explored cultural nuances.

Whenever I caught up with friends and acquaintances, they asked what I was up to with writing. It was the writer in me that they always remembered. They liked to point out that I was a seasoned writer and emotionally conscious wordsmith who astutely put into words the things unspoken across different cultures.

Despite my love for writing and encouragement around me, there was a point where I wanted to quit writing. Writing is not an easy craft. It takes a certain mindset and skills to keep writing. I wanted to walk away because writing felt incredibly difficult. Every step along the writing path felt like an obstacle.

This was exactly what I experienced when the demands across various writing projects accumulated. Freelancing full-time demanded a lot of my attention. I worked with clients on projects from personal branding to speech scripting, elevating their presence through the written word. There were countless late nights of back and forth with clients to figure out the clearest way to articulate their mission through memorable catchphrases.

Writing and posting about cultural nuances on my blog took time as well. It became a challenge to devote time to writing my book that I had started more than seven years ago. It is a book exploring the notion of belonging in culturally diverse settings, a book I was eager to publish. I was editing manuscript, refining the narrative arc and simply could not piece together the stories I wanted tell.

This was an incredibly challenging time for me as a writer. Not only was writing a difficult process in itself, there was minimal progress towards becoming a published author. I sincerely wanted to put in the effort for my clients, and for myself, as a writer. Yet it was a struggle to say what I wanted to say with words.

## The Difficulty with Writing

One reason writing can be difficult is because it requires tremendous patience. The process of writing often involves draft after draft before you see progress. It can feel like you are going round in circles when working towards precise wording, aligned grammar, concise language and desired flow in each manuscript. Such intensity that comes with repeated refining and playing with words to tell authentic stories is demanding, draining and adds up to more than a fair bit of time.

There is no guessing how many more redrafts you have in front of you before you see the finish line. Every late night I spent working with freelance clients left me wondering just how many more late nights of coming up with catchphrases there would be.

Writing is a highly mentally focused task that involves finding a balance between being clear and abstract with words. It requires the skill of blending the logic of grammar together with boundless creative tangents, crafting compelling stories that speak to readers. This is easier said than done, another reason writing is difficult.

It was no doubt challenging coming up with the right catchphrases that resonated with my freelance clients. It was even more challenging to find the right words describing my experiences caught in between Eastern and Western cultures as an Asian Australian when I redrafted my book.

Arguably just showing up as a writer is difficult. Good, compelling writing takes patience and time. Combined with finding the tenacity to blend logic and creativity within stories, that can make one tired writer. The longer I juggled freelance writing, blogging and editing my book, I was faced with keeping up writing proficiency. This slippery slope of creative burnout led to the pit of exhaustion: the more I wrote, the more I felt mental, physical and emotional drain as a writer.

In addition, writing is a solitary activity for most part which also makes it difficult. Some writers don't have others to turn to for support. Not everyone fully understands the writing process. With a lack of support, the writing road can be a lonely one. You wonder if the words you are cobbling together are relatable, let alone make sense. Your perspective is the only one you know.

On a cold and dark winter's night in Melbourne, I felt the most drained, tired and frustrated as a writer. As thankful as I was to write for others who saw worth in my words, it wore me down. Blogging wore me down. Figuring out the focus of my book wore me down.

As much as I enjoyed writing, on that night which felt so desolate, I didn't want to write anymore.

And that led me away from the path of writing, towards quitting writing altogether.

## Identity as a Writer

Writing for yourself and at your own pace is not immune to the difficulties of writing. The years of freelance writing and blogging began to wind down in the midst of my writing frustrations and difficulties. I had more time to redraft my book. Yet again I struggled to refine the narrative arc – it was like hitting a brick wall again and again.

I closed the draft of my book on my laptop. There was no

guessing when I was coming back to finish writing my book.

I no longer entertained writing projects or commitments. Quitting writing was real.

My friends, however, didn't think so and still thought I actively wrote. Shortly after this moment where I strayed from writing, a friend said, 'When you publish your book, you can travel the world and do book tours, speaking and meeting the people who bought your book!'

My friend enthusiastically believed in me as a writer who could go the distance as a best-selling author. However, the scenario she described felt so overwhelming and so far away for me as a self-professed introvert who dislikes the spotlight.

Writing is one thing and promoting your work is another thing.

My deep-thinking introverted mind went into a frenzy questioning my identity as writer up until that point.

*What if my writer's voice is lacking?*
*What if my story has already been told?*
*What if no one gets what I am writing in the first place?*

My friend's suggestion on promoting my writing reminded me of the difficulties of writing. There are many layers involved in the writing process. It's not surprising to feel inadequate as a writer amidst the difficulties.

An introverted personality is usually someone who gets energised from being alone and away from stimulating environments. It is generally someone who prefers reflection, deep conversations and meaningful perspectives.

Introversion can be an emphatic asset to writers. The bliss of solitary time can fuel passionate writing occasions. Diving into deep thoughts and exploring multiple plots can exhilarate.

But these same introverted traits can be obstacles to writing. Even though introverts enjoy alone time, the solitary activity of writing for months without support can drain. Countless hours of trying to get a manuscript 'just right' can result in frustration and negative self-talk. And perhaps even quitting.

As an introvert, to me staying in the struggles of writing was much more appealing than talking to readers and publishers and promoting my craft in public. While redrafting my book, I felt stuck deep in my deep thoughts, crippled by choices on which direction to steer the narrative arc. My perfectionist tendencies did not help either, with my inner voice telling me to persist redrafting until my manuscript felt complete.

Every writer has a unique writer's identity. The writer's identity draws on your personality, experiences, skills, groups you are a part of and more. It is your individuality that informs *who* you are as a writer and *how* you write. Notably there are different seasons in life. Amidst change in life, your writer's identity, what you write about and your approaches are likely to evolve. Part of the process of changing, developing and becoming a better writer often involves adopting a tougher, more resilient mindset.

## Writing Sabbatical

Historian David McCullough said, '*Writing is thinking. To write well is to think clearly. That's why it is so hard.*'

The difficulties of writing can make it incredibly hard to think clearly. You may be overwhelmed with the possibilities of telling your story and words elude you. You may be hard pressed to stay in a creative flow state when there are distractions around. You may be stressed from writing too much for too long.

In the months after walking away from writing, my world felt like a breath of fresh air. At first it felt strange as writing was an unequivocally part of my daily existence. But then the sense of overwhelm, intensity and stress from writing melted away.

I relished waking up to no deadline-pressing writing schedule, no more feeling under constant pressure. No more back and forth late nights with clients. No complex narratives running through my head a million miles an hour. No sitting in front of my laptop, staring at a blank page and writing just a paragraph over the next hour. No feeling deflated that that was the only progress I could make for the day as a seasoned writer.

I also relished time on my hands to do things I had put

off. I tidied the house, deep cleaning and organizing every room. I digitally decluttered the files on my laptop. I sorted my notebooks. Being the neat introvert that I am, such mundane organisational activities was refreshing.

The world of writing felt so far away, non-existent in fact. I was no longer exhausted and drained by the creative process. I looked forward to each day much more without the difficulties writing, emotionally feeling a sense of peace. It felt like I was me again, an organised introvert living a calm and composed lifestyle.

This was also an occasion where I had time to read more. I savoured the time to read for leisure instead of speed-reading for research on behalf of clients or solo writing projects. Some books I read captivated me from start to finish, transporting me to different worlds of different perspectives and advocating for something bigger.

The more I read, the more I appreciated what it takes to write and publish. Closing each book that I read, I pondered what makes a good book: compelling storylines, vivid imagery and elements of relatedness. A good book – and good writing – comprises intentional choice of words, natural flow of paragraphs and thoughtful characters. Then there's significant commitment in the form of long days and nights put into reviewing every sentence to achieve good writing.

Comparison is something many are guilty of but it also serves as a starting point for self-reflection and considering the next steps. Again I could not help but think about my writing journey so far. It has not been an easy road. But perhaps there is actually much to be gained from being a struggling artist.

And I toyed with the idea that perhaps, just perhaps, there was something in it for me with writing.

## Support and Other Perspectives

The more I reflected on what it takes to write well, the more I gained deeper perspective walking away from writing. It got me thinking about what makes a resilient, mentally tough writer.

From a psychological perspective, resilience relates to adapting in the face of challenges or coming back from adversity stronger than before. Looking beyond stress, acquiring skills, setting goals and making connections are some strategies that foster mental resilience. Resilience and the concept of mental toughness are related. Mental toughness is concerned with personality traits *together with positivity and confidence* adopted to deal with challenges. According to Professor Peter Clough, traits of mental toughness include feelings of control and commitment with a high level of self-belief – achievable through positive thinking, anxiety control and visualization.

For struggling writers, resilience could look like overcoming writer's block or returning to write after a sabbatical. For seasoned writers determined to enjoy writing for the long haul, perhaps having mental toughness looks like accepting creative frustrations and seeing the difficulties of writing as opportunities to improve one's craft.

During my time away from writing, I flipped through old notebooks where I had scrawled ideas for my book years ago. I reflected on my journey with a critical yet honest open mind. Perhaps my long-standing personal approaches contributed to my difficulties with writing. It seemed I took on too many writing commitments. I took on writing projects either to add to my portfolio or make a living. My writing geared towards a means to an end while writing out of passion was an afterthought, bringing weariness while pushing through.

Perhaps scaling back writing commitments would allow me to show up as writer more energetically and enthusiastically.

Perhaps carefully listing out each story idea or tangents with pen and paper would help me organise my tangled thoughts. By listing out each cool idea or wild tangent, I would probably see which ones connected with each other, making it easier to articulate words with both clarity and creativity.

Perhaps with better time management and adopting structured approaches towards writing, I would be a more patient writer.

Catching up with my friends who were writers provided added perspective while I was away from writing. We don't catch up often and talked in earnest on what we were writing. We talked about how redrafting a manuscript is such a frustrating process, how getting a book deal feels impossible and that self-publishing along with self-marketing can be a hard act to juggle.

One of my writer friends successfully published multiple fiction and graphic books over the years. He always had straightforward opinions about the writing process, and this time when we chatted was no exception.

We chatted about how it can be so difficult to get to the halfway point of writing a first manuscript. We talked about how so much time can go into deciding each part of a book, from the phrasing of one short sentence to the title. On getting stuck on a manuscript that he started, my friend offered a very honest yet simple approach, 'It's a bit like that. I might never finish what I started writing.'

I understood. There were tons of articles and manuscripts that I had started but never revisited for a second draft. The book that I am writing, well, I am not sure if it will ever see the light of day.

Connecting with empathetic fellow writers is a way to see the writing process more objectively. You see the writing habits or skills you can improve on. Your like-minded peers often help you confront your difficulties and see your work less negatively. The difficulties of writing feel normal.

Shortly after talking with my friend, my deep, wandering introverted mind entertained the thought of writing again. And the call to write beckoned to me again.

### Mental Toughness and Moving Ahead

The only writing which I kept up during my time away was the occasional blog post. Some posts were already written months ago. It really was a time where writing was the last thing on my mind.

As I began to have a different view of the writing process, the more I questioned my writing habits and patterns. And the more I thought about what to put into practice to address the difficulties of writing. Sometimes the next step forwards in the creative journey starts with positivity and self-belief.

Being composed and self-aware of personal emotional states led me towards a more intentional, steadier approach in showing up as a writer again. With a sense of calm stemming from my writing sabbatical, I sat down at my laptop. I read previous articles I wrote, finished and unfinished. Looking beyond the difficulties and stress of writing, I wondered where writing could actually lead me.

With quiet, solitary moments of deep thinking, I rationally planned the next steps in my writing path. No more freelance writing as it no longer resonated, just balancing blogging and book writing. Taking small steps back into the role of a writer, I felt a renewed focus and enthusiasm to write again.

Time away from writing allowed me to reset and regroup, to ground and develop mental fortitude. It reminded me of the bigger picture of why I write, and I write to encourage identities and exploring belonging.

With that goal clearly visualized and firmly in mind, I
felt a commitment and patience to pursue meaning
through the stories I craft as writer.

You can start anything on any day and pick up where you
left off another day. My time away from writing also
made me realise that there is often no need to rush.
Sitting down to edit the draft of my book once again, I
took my time rewording sentences. I seriously pondered
the structure of each chapter and the lessons of belonging
across cultures.

Returning to writing, I began to hone the skill of tuning
out the mental noise of self-doubt within me. Diving
deep into revising my book draft, I pushed away voices
in my head questioning my place and purpose as a writer.
I pushed away the thoughts that my writing is irrelevant
and focused on writing in the present moment. The more
I had no distractions, the more space I had to weave logic
with creativity within words.

Post writing sabbatical brought on a level-headed frame
of mind. I calmly yet firmly critiqued my writing with
detachment. Reading over my book on being 'too Asian
to be Australian and too Australian to be Asian', some
pages read as smooth as butter. But many of the
narratives written came across as unruly and needing
more thought. Some paragraphs made no sense at all.
Some sentences were confusing, others seemingly too
direct or defensive.

It felt time to be brutally honest about where my writing
was at. Reading through the entire manuscript, it felt like

my raw feelings and the stories I wanted to say were far from reflected in my words.

Every writer faces intimidating, vulnerable moments when questioning what they have written. It is times like these that compels change to become a better writer.

I did not like the draft of my book. What I had written did not resonate with me.

I took another look at my draft. This time I went over it more slowly, making notes on the sections that I wanted to rework. A few days later, I took yet another look at my draft and the notes. *It really, really needs work. A lot of work*, I thought, reminding myself of my writing goals, my creative composure and my strengths as an introvert.

I turned away from the draft, closing my laptop. I decided to start over writing my book from scratch. Starting over felt daunting. But I trusted that the introvert and writer in me had the resilience and toughness to move through rethinking, replanning and redrafting my book from the beginning.

## Wellness, Writing and Beyond

There is no formula for achieving personal wellness, and certainly no set formula for maintaining mental wellness as a writer. The concept of wellness is multi-dimensional and encompasses different dimensions of health: physical, mental, spiritual, emotional, social, and environmental wellness for example. In general, wellness is the active process of making choices, actions and activities towards optimal health. Regular habits and intentional lifestyles choices contribute to wellness, and towards wellbeing. Wellness and wellbeing are related concepts, with the latter regarded as the *state* of flourishing and optimal functioning where one feels (emotional, mental, psychological) satisfaction. Adopting the right approaches to wellness leads to optimal wellbeing.

As each person has different values, goals and desires, there are different variations towards cultivating wellness and therefore wellbeing. A person may also change approaches to wellness over time. For me, while mental dexterity and juggling multiple tasks comes naturally to me, taking on multiple time-consuming writing commitments was not sustainable alongside the difficulties of writing. So I quit writing – and thought I would never look back.

It was honest self-reflection during my writing sabbatical that minimized self-doubt. This helped me understand the importance of mental wellness and the habits to move through the difficulties of writing. That led to enjoying writing once again, even though if it meant vulnerably restarting a manuscript.

Building mental toughness and resilience played a vital part in cultivating wellness as a writer and encouraged me back on the path of writing. Adopting emotional composure, visualizing purpose and tuning out mental noise helped me show up as a patient writer and make the most of my skills. Connecting with fellow writers and playing to my strengths as an introvert helped nurture my identity as a writer and motivation to continue writing.

In addition, taking writing one step at a time might be the way to maintain mental wellness and make progress. That could look like focusing on writing a chapter of a manuscript in the present as opposed to wondering about the ambiguities of publishing down the track – which is when self-doubt and imposter syndrome kicks in.

It is important to look after oneself as a creative person, especially as a writer. Taking a break from writing is a chance to reset one's outlook, honing individual wellness and mental focus along the writer's path. It could be a thirty-minute break or longer sabbatical away from writing. Breaks allow rest, refocus and regaining composure, thinking clearly about what has been written so far. Instead of remaining stuck going around in circles rewording stories, you feel less stressed about writing and figure out the next steps with more perspective.

Many writers are excited in the early stages of writing ventures but the excitement can wane over time. Sometimes the more you write, the more uncertainty increases and you feel lost on your path as a writer. It's not surprising to feel overwhelmed by the difficulties of writing, leading to emotional snowballing and lack of creative motivation.

As with many creative endeavours, writing is a journey. That creative journey is likely to look different over time as wellness priorities shift. My writing journey has looked different throughout the years, and maintaining wellness too. From tirelessly juggling multiple writing projects to scaling back to writing projects that matter to me, there have been lessons learnt about mental resilience and toughness as a writer. Changing mindsets and approaches often helps in being a more a productive writer, including changing writing routines, content and the way you write.

Writing is difficult and there are times writers do actually quit. Sometimes taking a step back from writing encourages new perspectives and growth, and the ability to step forward with resilience and mental toughness on the creative road ahead. Sometimes it takes stepping back to assess and make willing changes towards the writer you are becoming, standing up to live before sitting down to write.

© Mabel Kwong 2023

.

*Different fuel.*

# CHAPTER THIRTEEN
## BLOGGING & REKINDLING
## BY MARSHA INGRAO

### Blogging: Rekindling the Splinters of Life

*"Every time you post something online, you have a choice. You can either make it something that adds to the happiness levels in the world—or you can make it something that takes away."*

~Zoe Sugg

### Blogging - A Public Journal or Something Else?

Tidbits of life splinter into a journal. Ninety-nine percent of it should never be swept into a pile and published. It is raw, unvarnished, and often boring or shocking. After my 36-year-old sister-in-law died, I found her journal stuffed in one of the dresser drawers in her room. Leslie's private thoughts had been off-limits to me when she was alive. She had never married and displayed few emotions beyond well-deserved complaints about her handicap and her bad health and fights with her mother, who she lived with.

But there it was. No thicker than an eighth of an inch, handwritten in ballpoint blue, carefully protected in a yellow three-pronged folder, the only real connection I would ever have with her. It intrigued me. What was she like inside?

## The Hidden Journal

### *Untitled*

*Jungle Jim, the Georgia peach,*

*Clobbers opponents within his reach.*

*With all that curly hair he's got,*

*Has he a permanent wave or not?*


*El Shereef, the bearded sheik,*

*He makes ringsiders yell and shriek.*

*Their remarks he seldom heeds,*

*but continues his nefarious deeds.*


*Arman Hussain is full of zeal.*

*And just as slippery as an eel.*

*Full Nelsons he can break with ease,*

*Although the crowd he's quick to please,*

*Opponents never think it's fun,*

*When by his skill, they are outdone.*

© Leslie Alvord circa 1965-1974

Leslie loved going to wrestling matches. Limping on uneven legs, using crutches fitted to her tiny arms, she attended alone and watched the men of steel entertain. She showed us a signed picture of one of them once.

Her journal contained a poem about Teddy (probably a wrestler), complete with a music score. She copied words from Scripture and a Johnny Mathis song, "A Certain Smile." Externally, she showed no signs of spirituality, creative expression, or musical interest. Internally, she had desires she kept hidden.

Why do I tell you all this? Writing is cathartic for people. They keep journals of lists, dates, poems, stories, music, drawings, inventions, gossip, and secret sins. As you read this, list what you might write in a journal. The expectation of a journal/diary is that no one will ever read it.

Leslie did not expect to die. Who expects a brain hemorrhage to hit you at age 36? She had few friends and certainly none that would be snooping in her drawers. It scared me that I would do such a thing, but I did. It is still in my file cabinet, and until now, I have never read beyond the first few pages. It felt sacred to me.

Throughout my 20-year first marriage, I kept journals, often getting up in the middle of the night to record poetry, my woes, or a flash of inspiration for my classroom. Unlike the famed diarist of *Mary Chestnut's Civil War*, my journals skimped on juicy news events and focused on grumbling, indiscretions, and selfishness.

**News Flash #1:** All the silent outpouring of my heart into stacks of notebooks never changed my attitude or my life situation.

My first husband became an assistant pastor eleven years into our marriage, giving me the dubious honor of becoming a pastor's wife. Pastors' wives are perfect, you know, or their congregations subconsciously expect them to be. In truth, they are growing or not growing at different rates, just like their congregants.

My first husband passed away at age forty-seven. The same recessive genetic problem, called Gaucher's Disease that caused his sister's aneurysm caused his death as well. Even though I was only forty-three, I became apprehensive that I might die unexpectedly, like Leslie. I worried that someone might discover the truth about me in the woodpile of shallow words scribbled at three in the morning, bemoaning a twenty-year marriage littered with financial woes, bouts of serious illness, and lack of intimacy. But they were part of me, and I could not let them go either. Isn't that weird?

When I remarried, I stuffed those honest revelations into a shredder, ripped from the spiral core page by yellowed page. Seeing scraps of crumbly newsprint reminded me that I did not want to ever indulge in a self-absorbed diary again, even ones with a list of books I read and wanted to read, poems, prayers, and lesson plans I designed. I also did not want to continue the same journey of unfulfilling, self-centered desires. For ten years, my journaling organically stopped.

**News Flash #2**: The creativity that journaling fostered inside me also started to wither.

## Traversing from Journaling to Blogging

As I neared retirement from teaching and consulting, I longed to follow the goal of my heart to write. Several friends suggested that I write a blog. Before I tried it, I started reading a friend's daughter's blog regularly. This young mother wrote about her work as a child and family photographer and her family, hobbies, and social life. Reading her blog was like reading a soap opera without sordid relationships. Her blog beguiled me but did not tempt me to become an engaged participant. I felt shy because I did not know her in real life. It shocked me that she was so open about her life and that many people commented on each post.

Some people vent on their blogs, but I did not want a public journal of the snags and splinters in my life. As Zoe Sugg suggested in the beginning quote, I chose to keep my blogging content and comments positive and leave my secrets in a private journal or not write them at all.

## Finding Reasons to Blog

> *"Blogging is an opportunity to connect with people and share your thoughts and ideas with the world."*
> ~ Darren Rowse

There are good reasons to start a blog. Many people use blogging to record their past, write a book, create a brand, enhance their career, sell products, travel logs, compete in challenges, entertain, educate, and inform. Unlike one friend who wrote news commentaries online, I did not have what I considered a good reason to blog.

When I started blogging, I was six months away from retirement. My life was moving along as smoothly as anyone else's on the highway of life. In my job, I had the opportunity to travel to attend meetings, not only across California but around the United States. I took a camera. I met intelligent, interesting people who became good friends. I wrote about my experiences.

My blog thrived on a different fuel than my lonely journals. Yet it served no unique purpose unless someone enjoyed reading life from a Californian teacher's perspective. I called my blog "Streaming Thoughts." Families and friends are not always interested in or have time to read day-to-day thoughts streaming across a white screen unless you have something helpful to say to them. I understood that close friends might not enjoy reliving bits and pieces of their lives filtered through my blog in the same way that my dad used to wear us out, showing slides of family trips or flowers in the yard whenever friends came over for an evening. (Boring!)

So how does someone without direction or significant reason to blog find something meaningful to write? Frankly, I floundered. I had to learn to write something that strangers would want to read. For the first time, my writing had to be marketable. I did not realize it then, but I had become a publisher and writer.

Day after day, like a new swimmer, I never wanted to get out of the internet pool. Blogging took me into the "deep end" of social media. I established Facebook, LinkedIn, Tumbler, and Twitter accounts because my blog posts appeared in my social media feeds after they went live. Frantically, I tried to stay current on all of them. I dog-paddled harder and harder without having a clue about what I should write.

My blog tumbled around, looking for a place in the blogosphere.

- At first, I told silly stories from my past.
- Since I traveled extensively, I shared pictures from trips with commentary.
- I played the awards game, answering questions and linking to other blogs. These posts reminded me of receiving chain letters when I was a kid. They were cheesy but connected me to people I would never have met. They also challenged me to discuss topics that I would not have approached.
- I discovered photo and writing challenges

which linked me to more bloggers.

- Being the sage on the stage, writing about blogging, photography, organization, and time management, and writing appealed to me. I found that I knew much less than I thought I knew.
- Writing about education, my profession, seemed too much like work, so out of over sixteen-hundred posts, I tagged only fourteen posts about that topic.

Any number of readers besides myself was a considerable improvement in followers of my writing. Several people started corresponding with me regularly. Blogging hooked me and became an experiment or hobby.

## Speaking of Education and Learning

*"The best time to act on this was decades ago. The second-best time is now."*
~David Brin

As an educator, I provided professional development for math, language arts, and history teachers. Even though I worked hard at my writing tasks as a teacher and consultant, I should have learned to blog first.

In my job as an educational consultant and classroom teacher coach, research, reading, and writing were the skills of my trade. I scored well on achievement and credentialing tests in writing. I taught writing to students and adults so they could do the same. The goal was not for my students to produce published works that would draw worldwide readers. They learned how to answer prompts to pass tests. Since I was not a published author of any genre, I had no idea how different those writing skills were than what I taught.

One of my early readers asked me what I learned from blogging. Even though I had a master's degree in Curriculum and Instruction and an Administrative Credential, I had much to learn as a writer and communicator.

And the coaching skills I had used in education? Who pops into the lives of bloggers worldwide and consults about their blogs? As it turned out, years after I started up my blogging path alone, the solitary life began to disappear, as I will share later.

Blogging started as an experiment. I read books and hundreds of articles on blogging. I learned things like:
- A new vocabulary
- Write shorter paragraphs.
- Create catchy titles.
- Include pictures or art.
- Develop a niche or purpose for the blog.
- Write consistently.
- Respond to people.
- Construct an attractive page.
- Use online proofreading tools.
- New forms of poetry
- Technical photography and photo processing skills

Beyond the technical skills, blogging also developed soft skills in my life. Soft skills are those skills that you cannot measure with statistics and tests. Teachers are aware of the soft skills that their students develop, like how to work cooperatively in a group or make friends. In blogging, too, soft skills are more critical than the competencies you can assess - how many views, likes, and followers.

I have friends in real life (IRL) who do not blog and did not believe that I could be close to my blogging friends. But nothing could be farther from the truth.

When someone reads and comments on my blog, I read their blog and write a comment. Genuine relationships develop. We exchange tips on everything from where to travel, to what to look for in good realtors, and how to deal with the death of a spouse.

Within two or three months after I began blogging, I was on a constant emotional high.

- People listened and responded to my writing and my developing photography hobby.
- As a blogger, **I did not interrupt or struggle to express my ideas** as I had in meetings. In fact, I could not interrupt. Blogging is linear. You write, then wait for a response - sometimes for days, then write again.
- I developed confidence and new skills, which inspired me to blog at all hours of the day. My husband said that I quit sleeping to blog.

In the fifteen years of our marriage, before I blogged, Vince rarely asked me about my job. Because I enjoyed and understood his work as a realtor and loved looking at houses, we naturally talked more about his work and interests than mine.

It thrilled me when he started reading my posts on Facebook. He found my mistakes and told me when he liked my post and my pictures. We began talking more about my world. Sometimes I blog about Vince's world, and he glows. He wants to see what my friends say about his world. Our worlds are connected in a fuller way than before I shared my writing publicly.

Last summer Vince and I met Terri Webster Schrandt's brother-in-law who helps us manage our condominium in Scottsdale when we need it. I learned which teeth whitening strips work best at our last blogger meetup. You cannot measure those skills with Google Analytics.

If I had an entire book, I could not complete a list of all the soft skills that blogging developed in me.

## Blogging Beyond Experimentation

> *"You can buy attention (advertising). You can beg for attention from the media (PR). You can bug people one at a time to get attention (sales). Or you can earn attention by creating something interesting and valuable and then publishing it online for free."*
> ~David Meerman Scott

At one point, Vince thought I should expand and make

money from my blog. I tried, I really did, but my heart was never in it. In case you are interested, Forbes published a post in the early years of blogging explaining twenty-five ways to monetize a blog. Bloggers can earn thousands of dollars with their blogs. I netted about ten dollars over the year that I tried to make my blog pay as an affiliate of Amazon. One company hired me to write four content articles about products. I earned about two hundred dollars for those. They never appeared on my blog.

I wrote a post about a business in Woodlake, CA, which was one hundred years old. A publisher from South Carolina contacted me and asked if I wanted to write a book about Woodlake. At first, I thought it was a scam, but I took the plunge and said yes to writing the book.

My lifetime dream of becoming an author came true after five months of ten-hour days, over forty interviews, collecting hundreds of pictures, writing, and editing for historical and grammatical accuracy. I was a published book author and a big name in the small town of Woodlake.

Writing a book took me on a journey I could never have imagined. In my mind, I was a behind-the-scenes person collecting recollections, writing in my study, and gathering opinions to help me make the tough decisions as to which events were important in the over one-hundred-year-old life of this town.

Even though it was a small town of only seven thousand people, my book thrust me into the limelight. In 2016 I was honored as the "Woodlake Woman of the Year." To be honest, I did not have the requisite skills to accept the recognition with poise. I talked too long at the banquet and tried to give credit to everyone who had shared their photos and knowledge with me. They practically had to drag me off the stage. I know I flushed bright red for at least six months.

## Speaking of Making Friends

My blogging friends followed me on Facebook, too. My first blogger meetup was with a man from San Diego named Russel Ray, a photographer. I met him on one of my trips with my history consultant friends.

Around the same time, two blogging friends from Australia and I started video chatting. Carol and I enrolled in an online class to learn how to write children's books. Leanne Cole gave me photography lessons through FB Chat. She taught me what you could do with Camera Roll (Raw). Learning to understand her accent baffled me as did the digital photo processing techniques and vocabulary. Yet, I persisted as she took me to a new level of photography! As I learned new skills, I became the one who was coached rather than the coach.

Soon we had to meet, first here in the U.S.A. A mere four years after I began my blog, I flew to Australia alone in December 2016, to meet both of my Aussie friends. In my wildest dreams, I would never have pictured myself going to Australia.

I have been honored to meet thirteen bloggers face-to-face from New England to Australia.

## Cresting the Blog

> *"Blogging is like work, but without coworkers thwarting you at every turn."*
> ~ Scott Adams

Of course, experiences in life besides blogging built my skill levels and brought me to the point where I began blogging. Though I am far from perfect, I honor and thank God for the talents, skills, opportunities, patience, and forgiveness that have come my way. My parents and family, including both of my husbands supported but never pushed me. My jobs and career stretched me out of the shy shell I occupied as a child.

No one starts any endeavor as an expert. Nor do skills from one occupation or hobby necessarily transfer to other ventures. However, I want to remind you again about the young woman who journaled alone at night. That woman never thought she would publish a book, poem, article, or anything. Now I have published at least one of each and thousands of blog posts.

Blogging helped change me into a more public, community-oriented person. Post-retirement opportunities that resulted from blogging skills:
- President of the California Council for the Social Studies (CCSS)
- Secretary of Kiwanis of Woodlake,
- Secretary of the Woodlake Chamber of Commerce,

- Museum Committee member as Woodlake established its first museum.
- Maintained social media accounts for CCSS and its local affiliate, the San Joaquin Valley Council for the Social Studies (SJVCSS), Kiwanis, and the Woodlake Chamber.
- Woodlake representative on the Sequoia Tourism Council.
- Concerned citizen for the protection of the Woodlake Botanical Garden group called Woodlake Pride, and I started a blog for the Garden.
- Wrote the monthly church newsletter.

In August 2015, Arcadia Books published *Images of America Woodlake.* My blog was well established, and I had completed about 100,000 words in my fiction attempt, *Girls on Fire.* I hoped my writing career would be on fire. Vince kept his fingers crossed for a movie deal when I finished. An editor felt differently and urged me to read Liane Moriarty's books. I loved them, and at least one of her books became a popular series. *Girls on Fire* moved to a back burner on the campfire.

I wore out about six years after I started my first blog. I slowed down near the peak of my blog's success, where most bloggers settle into their routines. My money-making blog, "Always Write," had been an experimental flop. The blogs and social media accounts I ran for others dragged behind me like a chain. I was ready to quit blogging my fun blog, "Streaming Thoughts." I told my friend Sally how exhausted I was and wanted to delete my "Always Write" blog. Even though she was not a blogger, she urged me not to do it.

"At least copy the content," she said. I took her advice but blogged very little during 2018 and 2019. What I did not know was that I had developed breast cancer. I had noticed a slight indentation; a mammogram discovered it buried deep while it was still small and in stage one.

## Developing a Rhythm in Life

> *"Don't focus on having a great blog. Focus on*
> *producing a blog that's great for your readers."*
> ~ Brian Clark

Out of the billions of bloggers worldwide, many drop out once, several times, or permanently during their lives. Many take breaks and slow down to a pace they can manage. When I started blogging more regularly in 2020, most of my former friends had faded into the web.

No longer was blogging an experiment for me. However, I still needed to redefine myself as a blogger and figure out what I enjoyed most about it as well. In addition, I still needed to figure out a way to serve others, not just my own needs.

My blog could have become an opportunity to talk about my breast cancer experience. I walked away from that direction in blogging for the same reasons I chose not to write a blog about education. Even though I felt gratitude toward the Lord for all the excellent doctors and nurses and what having cancer did for me spiritually, I did not want illness to be the focus of my blog. I mention it occasionally, but it is not the focus of my life or my blog.

Because I had always enjoyed photo challenges, when I returned to a consistent blogging schedule, I turned to Cee Neuner's blog. She had been hosting challenges since I started blogging and was still at it eight years later. I put my best efforts into writing posts that answered her challenges. Challenge examples were:

- Find or take pictures with predominant lines, colors, circles, and squares.
- Color challenges – pictures with one or two prominent colors
- Bridges, Doors, Trios, Windows, Reflections, Sunsets, Rain, Snow, anything that flies, Benches, and Trees
- Find pictures that illustrate an idea: Up, Soft, Twisted, Unique
- Find pictures that illustrate a technique like Bokeh, Perspective, Rule of Thirds

You get the idea. It is like being a pharmacist filling a photo prescription. Writing challenges are similar:

- Write a poem about Spring, Love, or a Picture.
- Write a 99-word story about a Dog, Loss, Falling, or Climbing
- Write a story or poem of any length using specific words.

Then it hit me. Participating in challenges of all sorts was what I enjoyed about blogging. In mid-2020, I began to interview challenge hosts. By publishing interviews on my blog, I could benefit the hosts and the participants, and I would learn something, too.

Starting on June 30, I began interviewing challenge hosts. I would pour over their blog, ask them questions by email and write a post. We were three months into the Pandemic. Soon, I began Zooming with them as part of the interview process. Accents from around the world hit my ears, but the fantastic thing was that it seemed like I had known these bloggers for a long time.

Cee Neuner started a small group of us Zooming each week to get to know each other better. Baby pictures, husbands, dogs, cats, decor, crazy Zoom backgrounds, and talk about our blogs, the weather, health, and the Pandemic, and photography took personal blogging to a greater depth of intimacy.

Zooming was such fun. Best of all, we shared expertise and were not blogging alone with YouTube videos for instruction. Blogging was less lonely when we started meeting each other. Remember that I had been a coach for teachers. Now I have the expertise to coach bloggers, and they also coached me.

Cee also helped me develop my first photo challenge. She co-hosted *Photographing Public Art Challenge* for a while before she cut me off to fly on my own. A guest blog post with Hugh Roberts became another challenge called *Story Chat*. Challenge host blogger Colleen

Chesebro gave me the privilege of hosting a challenge she and another blogger hosted four years before called *Writer's Quotes Wednesday Writing Challenge*.

In addition to Zoom interviews, bloggers planned meetups in our geographic areas. Even though I did not attend, I read about blogging conventions and blogger bashes all over the world. We now have a group that varies from two to eight of us and sometimes includes visitors and spouses. Our vibrant group set a goal to meet monthly somewhere in Arizona for lunch and photo field trips.

Sometimes bloggers travel quite a distance to meet. Initially, Terri Webster Schrandt and I met when we lived in California. In the fall of 2022, we planned a meetup in Portland, Oregon. She drove from Spokane, and I flew from Prescott, AZ. We spent an amazing ten days together, meeting with other bloggers from the Northwest along the way. In our spare time, we challenged each other to take more compelling pictures and competed to see who could get in the most steps each day on our Fitbits.

Even though I still only host one other challenge, now called *Wednesday Quotes*, Yvette Prior, one of the *Story Chat* authors, invited me to co-host the *Dickens Challenge* this year, highlighting five of his novellas. She also honored me by asking me to be part of this book, *This Is How We Grow*, and I am so excited to be alive and part of this work.
New avenues of blogging keep opening.

# Conclusion

*"Blogging is just writing — writing using a particularly efficient type of publishing technology."*

~ Simon Dumenco

In my life, blogging is an essential daily activity. While it is not my only source of growth and healing, it has dramatically augmented my life and enabled me to be creative and benefit others. Writing posts and comments keeps me fit mentally, emotionally, and spiritually. It has helped me focus on positive thoughts and actions through two major health crises - cancer and the deadly combination of having deep vein thrombosis, pulmonary emboli, and pneumonia at the same time.

Years ago, someone shared a diagram with our Migrant Education staff that explained there are four parts to our personalities or spirits. Thirty years later, I still remember the basics from that lesson. The speaker drew a box dividing our beings into private and public parts. Then she talked about who could see which part of us.

On the public side of me in square #1, my readers see the parts of me that I care to share, my public "Facebook Persona" online. Blogging, as in real life, reveals only part of us - the part we choose to display. No matter how open we seem to be, we do not share everything with others. Our public side in blogging is as authentic as our public persona in our face-to-face life, but writing allows us to philosophize and let people see our thoughts at a deeper level. My blog is my legacy to the world.

Square #3 of the four-part diagram describes another aspect of my public self, the Marsha that others see. My readers, like those who observe me as I go about my work and play, also make observations based on comments, reading between the lines, and looking at pictures. They develop their view of me, which I can only see if they share it. They might even talk behind my back!

The two private quarters mean that either others cannot see into that section of our lives, or we cannot see it. Our journals might reveal what no one else can know about us until we die. I want to keep my private thoughts confidential. Journals in which I disclosed troubled thoughts are long gone.

The final private section of our spirit or soul is one that no one can see except a higher being I call God. Our total potential, our true raison d'être, what will happen to us – good and bad and our responses to those events is not information we are privileged to know.

As people age, some complain that they can no longer do what they once did. They are out of sorts, irritable, and begin to live in the past. Bloggers, on the other hand, always have something new to read, learn and write. We can be creative and productive until we can no longer press the keys or use a voice recognition program to publish our thoughts.

I have grown past groaning into a private journal. My journals are now guidebooks for the work I must do.

No longer am I to be ashamed that someone will read my words after I am gone, for my blog shows growth and reveals only the amount of my life I choose to publish. I update it consistently to keep it viable. At the same time, I have found a niche, a reason to write, so that my blog provides a service to encourage both bloggers and non-bloggers.

I hope my story will bring you encouragement for your healing and growth as well.

### Perspective As a Bridge

My life, my pleasure,
feet, cars crossing my pavement,
Safety over the abyss,
The gentle stream far below.

I smiled down at the stream,
A mere babbling brook
bounding over boulders
Caressing the banks with butterfly kisses.

This morning I awoke in pain,
My limb useless and shattered
by my dear stream gone rampant,
Sticks and stones breaking my bones.

I lay helpless in frigid waters,
Pouring over my cement skin,
Ripping and tearing at my guardrails,
I cry out a warning, my voice muted by turbulence.

Friendly waters turned explosive,
Silky snowflakes joining force,
Taking me down to my grave,
My years of service ended abruptly.

*©Marsha Ingrao, 2023 Free Verse using Personification.
I wrote this poem in response to a writing challenge after
a flood in California covered a bridge over the creek that
runs behind what was once our backyard.*

## Untitled
Waterdrop patterns
Cling to fragile spring petals
Satisfy their thirst.
*©Marsha Ingrao, 2023
Traditional Haiku, Based on a photo taken at
Allensworth State Park, California, 2006*

## What to Do with Poems
I'm collecting them,
One by one in a binder,
As I write them.
I think they're great.
Then I read someone else's poem,
And I head back to the computer,
To write another poem,
Which I'm collecting,
One by one, in a binder,
As I write them.
*© Marsha Ingrao 1998 Free Verse*

© Marsha Ingrao 2023

*Right one moment, wrong the next.*

# CHAPTER FOURTEEN
## RIGHT AND WRONG
## BY CADE PRIOR

How to view the world through a lens which creates more empathy and compassion for others.

Through the process of reading this, you will subconsciously judge each sentence, underline its meaning, and evaluate each description, asking yourself if what I am saying is "right" or "wrong".

Before reading this, you already have ideas about what is right and wrong in your own life.

Five years from now, you will, hopefully, have different views on what is "right" and "wrong".

So, what *is* right and wrong? If our views change and something can be right one moment and wrong the next, **then what is it truly?** How can something be right for one person and wrong for another?

This comes down to the truth that **there is no such thing as absolute right and wrong.** There is even a paradox within that sentence.

Right and wrong are human constructs that were developed in our brains through the process of evolution with the main goal of survival. We judge right and wrong because right meant survival, and wrong meant death, pain, or suffering. Our bodies and brains are hardwired to see things from the lens of right and wrong (black and white) because natural selection favored those who chose "the right" decision.

Nowadays, survival is less of a concern. We have the modern-day version of it, but many of our "wrong" decisions don't cost us our lives (although some can and do).

The simple fact is this: "Right" and "wrong" are **an individual's perspective based on their *objectives* and values.**

Here's an example of how this plays out in the real world. To a zebra, death is "bad" because it's viewing the world from the perspective of a zebra, and it has its own individual objective, which is to survive.

The goal of a lion, however, is similar, but its rights and wrongs are different. It eats zebras for its survival. So in the event that a zebra were to die by the lion, the lion would view the situation as "good," while the zebra would view the situation as "bad." However, in this example, maybe the objective of nature is for both animals to die. The bodies will eventually decompose into fertilization for the soil which is "good" in nature's view.

Events within themselves are neither good nor bad. They are simply events. It's only the perspectives and objectives of an individual that make an outcome right or wrong.

Another example that I love to give is imagining an intelligent being that created and observes the entire universe. His goal in making the universe was to create planets without life. He would then view planets with life as wrong. He would view our earth as moldy, an infection, or a "faulty" planet. To him, human existence would be wrong.

We humans tend to view things like this on a similar scale. To an infection that has invaded our human body and made us sick, the infection is doing what is right. To us, and our objectives, we view that as wrong. But the truth is, it is neither right nor wrong.

We, as human beings, have trouble seeing this because, well, it is not beneficial for our survival to think and theorize about others' rights and wrongs. And if we did, natural selection would favor those who only cared about their rights and their tribes/families' rights and wrongs.

*Side note: There's a very interesting concept within the greatest "wrongdoings" that have been done in the world, by people like serial killers, wars, etc. The individuals committing these heinous acts do not, in their minds, believe they are doing something wrong. There is an idea in psychology that no one intentionally does wrong, and when they do, somewhere in their brain, they think it is "right". So even the worst of acts have some underlying "rightness" to them.*

So what does this mean? Well, it means quite a lot.

1. You are foolish to judge people, viewing what they do as right or wrong. Who are you to say? You can only say what is right and wrong for yourself. (With the exception of shared *objectives, which we will discuss*)
2. What is right and wrong will change as your goals in life change. So holding any belief is foolish as you will likely have different goals.
3. You may be misinformed. I will dive into this more, but this is the basis for "The best-intentioned, worst person."
4. God has a right and wrong that is different from ours. If you believe in something higher than you, you must trust that your rights and wrongs are nothing compared to theirs. And you might be destined to a life of "wrongs" for the benefits of someone else's rights. This is an unfortunate truth that most people don't want to accept.

5. If you feel unhappy, that is a sign that you are making "wrong" decisions based on your true objectives/human objectives.
6. As human beings, we do share similar rights and wrongs because we all have similar objectives. (Drinking water is "right" for human beings because our objective is to live, and without it, we would die.) This is what we call "Human Needs."
7. Getting clear on your overall objective for your life will help you make better decisions because it's the basis for judging what is "right and wrong."

Even the worst acts on earth - to some degree, are neither wrong nor right. It is the judgment of an individual based on their perspective and objectives that defines it, to them.

**Seeing others perspectives.**

When we understand what was stated above, seeing others' perspectives becomes a little more interesting. We no longer look at actions from a place of judgement and criticism for how they live, because who are we to say they are doing something wrong. There are arguments, however, that human beings share objectives which could classify certain actions as absolute rights or wrongs. Yet once again, why we would we focus on others when we instead can focus on our definition and God's definition of right for our lives.

Now, let's discuss applying this information to benefit your life - and the life of others around you.

## How do I apply this information?

Even though I believe there are no such things as absolute rights and wrongs, it can be VERY beneficial to view life through the right and wrong lens. If we didn't, we wouldn't be here, and you would be at serious risk for death and pain every day.

We can say things like drinking and driving is "wrong" because human beings share the objective to live. Statistically, drinking and driving is incredibly dangerous and illegal. We can, therefore, say it is **wrong** for one to do so.

But what about the less obvious things? What about smaller choices, like making your bed, living in this location vs. that location, etc.?

It all comes down to becoming clear on whether that decision truly pushes you towards your objectives. And becoming very clear on what I call "unknown objectives," which are the greatest cause of regret.

*Example:* A very common myth in the world of health is that red meat is bad for you. And if you are reading this and you believe that, I am here to tell you you're wrong... Kidding. Who am I to say? ;)

However, with that being said, there is a lot of new information, scientific studies, meta-analyses, and anecdotal evidence to show that the negative health claims about red meat were incorrect – they were wrong. Eating red meat, daily, might not be as bad for us as we

284

thought. It actually might be the right for humans and as a notorious source of fuel, it could be the key to thriving and attaining optimal health.

If this is true, then everyone who had the objective to be healthy, because of information decided that going vegan was healthy, they would in this context be wrong. It could also be true that because we are different, for some people, this is wrong, and for some people, this is right. However, this disregards the fact that there are human basic human survival needs that we all share, like drinking water. No matter how different we are and no matter how we view a preference, the human body has very specific needs.

Many times in our life, we will be wrong. We will be misinformed, we will draw conclusions that after more information is presented, we realize we are point-blank, WRONG.

So this means that in order to make good decisions, we must first get clear on our objectives in life. We must know what we are working towards. And we must become informed as to what will help us reach that objective.

**This means that open-minded people have a higher chance of achieving their goals.**

I am in absolute favor of being open-minded. You may even notice in the process of reading this you have judgment towards what I'm saying based on what you believe is right and wrong. While it's completely natural, and ironic considering the topic, try your best to remove any judgements and beliefs, see it for what it is, simply words on a page - which may help you towards your *objectives.*

We must be open-minded. Even I, writing this, understand that my ideas may, and hopefully will, change. I want them to change because the key to achieving our objectives in life is to adjust our outlook, have a growth mindset, and do our best to make good decisions. If I am clear on my objectives and aware of my biases as a human, then the missing piece must be information on what will truly push me towards my goals or push me away from them.

Therefore, each decision I make must be, to the best of my knowledge at the time of making it, the right decision based on my goals. While at the same time, understanding that new information may come my way, which can then change whether I view that decision as right or wrong.

Many times when we experience regret, we experience it for two reasons.

1. We realize the decision we thought would push us towards our goals was actually pushing us away from them. The problem of being misinformed and sometimes closed-minded. This can create what I noted earlier was "a well-intentioned, terrible person."
2. Our objectives change. We originally had an objective, and we were making right decisions

based on that objective. But later in life, our objectives change. Or we realize we never even wanted that objective. Therefore, based on our new objective/goal, we view our decisions as "wrong." Sometimes, it's also related to issues of having buried, or deep down objectives, and not realizing you had them - until it's too late.

We see this all the time in the world. People have an objective to make money or become very successful. If that is the goal, and the only goal, a lot of decisions like neglecting your family, working 80 hours a week, etc., become "right" decisions.

But later in life, we realize we had other objectives. We had other things we wanted to accomplish. And those right, or good, decisions, despite them helping us achieve our goals, were actually out of alignment with our true goals and values.

So not only do you have to be clear on your objectives in life, **you better hope you get them right.** Need to hope that they are truly what you want. You better hope you don't fail to see an objective you truly have because it could lead to regret; it could lead to feeling like you made wrong decisions in your short-lived life. And you better hope that you don't put all of your "good" decisions into the wrong objective, which we see many people do often.

We are human beings. We share similar objectives. It is foolish and can lead to guaranteed regret if we pretend that we do not have shared objectives as human beings. These are known as human needs.

These shared objectives (although there are exceptions) are things like health, happiness, contentment, meaning, challenge, fulfillment, survival, etc.

While there are people who don't care about these things, I would argue that because they are still human, they still have these as deep down goals. Deep down, they have these *objectives*.

If that were true, then some form of our decisions need to be guided by these objectives; therefore, a lot of work should be done to clarify wrong aims and reach right objectives.

Therefore, in conclusion, even though I believe there are no absolute rights and wrongs, there are individual rights and wrongs. And these are beneficial not only for survival but also for achieving what we want in life. People who make "wrong decisions" are usually not clear on their objectives (and have hidden objectives) and/or they are misinformed, which can almost guarantee a life with more regret. Becoming clear on your true objectives, staying open-minded, and educating yourself with information are the key lessons one can learn from reading this chapter.

## A thought on trusting nature:

*You are foolish to believe you have insight as to what "should" and what "should not" happen to you. Why do you think you know how life should go? Why do you think that you have the universal truth between right and wrong?*

*It is freedom in knowing that no matter what comes your way, this is natures plan. This is God's plan. Nature knows best. For we are limited in what we know and biased as to what we think.*

*We can free ourselves, if we understand our limitations and understand the importance of every experience (good or bad).*

*For when we accept the truth, and stop trying to force things unnaturally, nature can step in and fulfill its destiny for you. It's in this moment that you can use everything that happens to you to your advantage.*

*It is in our greatest and darkest moments that create the person we're destined to become. Do not force what is not meant to be.*

© Cade Prior 2023

*See what you see.*

# CHAPTER FIFTEEN
## CLOSING THOUGHTS
## BY YVETTE PRIOR

We hope that you found a few takeaways from reading the stories and poems in this book. We also hope that you remember it can take a long time to understand our mental filters, bias, and blind spots. The effort is worth it because it can lead to a better you and a more fortified society. Problem-solving with a growth mindset and letting life's lessons lead to enjoyable fruits can lead to satisfying moments.

Your hardest day might not have arrived yet. Your toughest challenge in life could still be coming and will you be able to see it through? I hope so. I also hope the stories and poems in this book become sprouts of hope during any future challenges that come your way. We need to monitor our growth through individual wellness and by having peace in our life.

Each chapter in this book had variety and flavor with an individual expression of ideas. We aimed to use personal content to transmit important cultural information and values from one individual to the next and I hope this goal was reached.

After you close this book, may you always remember that your outlook will change because it is part of human growth. Cade reminded us that our mental filters will change as the way we view right and wrong will change too. As we learn more about individual bias, conditioning, and faulty thinking, we need to pay attention to other people's viewpoints and stay open to information that is incongruent with our current mental filters.

Sherri let us feel some California and English culture fusion, with reminders about how close and connected we all are in this big ol' world. Let's remember this when we feel a spirit of division. Can we put aside what divides and remember that we have more in common than we might not initially see? The butterfly effect came to mind as Sherri showed us that people are connected by a maximum of six steps. She also made us smile with the timeless reminder to *always remember to call your mother*.

We hope that you smiled to imagine Miriam and her husband enjoying ample time with grandchildren as they reestablished roots in new soil. We also felt Miriam's experience of going from having no grandkids, to getting the joyful news, to then having the pandemic limit travel to see their growing family. They eventually were able to live nearby family and her chapter left us with uplifting familial warmth.

Ana let us feel unfolding family love as she shared about perspective changes and generational connections. She also demonstrated that the capacity to adopt the perspective of someone else can take time. Ana shared about her aunt, who had the middle name of Dragonfly, and the way Ana described a dragonfly reminded me of human perspective: "beautiful and ugly, delicate and strong, graceful and maladroit, and also with a paradox of antagonistic features." The components of perspective and empathy are intertwined and complex, just like Ana's Aunt Dragonfly was.

You might leave this book feeling satisfied with the way Marsha's blogging experience eventually led to soft skill development, friendship, life fuel, and a way to offer customized outreach. Marsha's *Perspective as a Bridge* poem gave us an analogy for life's changes with the changing water. The gentle stream and babbling brook became turbulent and began ripping and tearing the guardrails. Problems can come our way like that. When storms come, we do the best we can to respond, cope, stay stable, and grow.

Lauren explored the topic of outlook with views about body image. Keri's story reminded us that empathy consists of both affective and cognitive components. Growing with understanding also requires mental flexibility and self-regulation. Unconsciously, we learn to associate certain attributes, like weight, with social identities and potential bias for what society says is trendy and ideal. Lauren reminded us that we cannot keep doing the same thing and expect different results so let's all keep exploring mental filters and bias.

Mabel's chapter reminded us that individual wellness unfolds as we keep moving on our journey.

Mabel gained a deeper perspective by pausing or walking away from, writing, which made a huge difference in her affect and outlook. Life is not always easy and the obstacles she had with her writing provide a reminder for us to all *stay the course* and find what we need to do to stabilize and cultivate wellness.

Robbie shared her growth over six years as she dealt with illnesses with both of her children. Some of the details about doctors, and how they ended up finding some solutions to the health challenges, are good examples of how it can take investigative work to fully see what is going on. Robbie also let us feel how vulnerable and raw the health challenges were yet the experiences also came with silver linings. The beauty is there if we put forth the effort to see it.

Jeff let us feel layers of vulnerability as well. His poems brought us into his social world and the ups and downs he has had over the years. He has adapted to different living arrangements, with continuous intentional behaviors, to find joy whether he has to anchor down or move around. One of his poems mentioned boundaries that were set in place to keep his soul in peace. May we all learn to do that for our growth and wellness.

Trent's story led us through action and I enjoyed feeling the splashes of water near the end of the story. Perhaps some of us could relate to the relief that came with finally discovering that assumptions were wrong. We humans not only tend to have wrong assumptions, but those wrong assumptions are often negative too. Maybe we can start assuming the best and clarify sooner to minimize distorted thinking.

Mahesh let us feel humor as he talked about words and accents while he also took us down his experience with the history of the Internet. The current digital world is something many of us take for granted but it had to grow, evolve, and mature over many years. Humans are similar in how it takes time to understand and a behavior he once perceived as snobby "wasn't a show-off but rather an unending work in progress." Mahesh reminds us that cultural identity is a living organism that expands, morphs, and underpins perspective and outlook.

Developing empathy takes more time for some people and some folks, like my dear ol' father-in-law, might not have low empathy because they have a progressive disorder that impairs perspective-taking. But even people who have symptoms of a personality disorder can grow and improve. Their growth might be very slow and strained, but it can occur – as we saw when our daddio made some progress in his final years. Truth about cognitive biases finally reached him and he slowly began to reframe and adjust some of his assessments. It was gratifying to see his growth in those final years while he was also so humbled from needing more and more caregiving.

Speaking of caregiving, Mike's chapter offered tips and advice for surviving and thriving while in caregiver mode. The physical exhaustion and mental drain *can* be mitigated. Mike's chapter also let us into his personal life as he shared about how it took time for him to understand relationship dynamics and then live out what he had advised in a clinical setting. This reminded me that so much of life is about learning as we go. We can prevent some problems but not all of them. The goal is to learn about coping so that we can manage, cope, process, heal, and move forward with health.

## This is How we Grow

Sometimes the only way we learn and develop maturity is through the megaphone of pain or from a major setback. Other times we might grow from a nudge or small trial as we are easily shaped from an experience. However, there is another way to grow and expand insight, which is proactive and involves using the art of perspective-taking. Reading stories and poems, like the ones in this book, can help us identify diverse points of view and better understand people with more profundity. Perspective-taking can also involve watching shows, documentaries, movies, listening to podcasts, or joining groups that allow us to leave our comfort zone.

There are so many ways to improve and expand outlook and the goal is to at least try to better understand self and others.

## About the Authors

Yvette Prior, contributing author and editor for this anthology, works as a university professor and conducts research. After earning a PhD in Industrial & Organizational Psychology, she poured into book projects and she is currently working on a Cognitive Psychology handbook. Her past work experience has included teaching art, counseling, hospitality management, and doing outreach. Yvette finds refreshment from yoga, exploring the arts, and blogging at priorhouse.wordpress.com

Ana Linden is currently a translator, but she also put her BA in Foreign Languages and Literature to good use by teaching… once upon a time. Reading and writing have always provided her with solutions and answers. She is the author of *Parallel Lives, Glass Slippers and Stilettos, Albatross, Frames* and *Christmas Reunion*. Ana is also and the voice behind various stories and musings on her personal blog analinden.wordpress.com. Nevertheless, most of her writing is for her eyes alone. Were life to be a dream come true, she would spend a good part of her time traveling, reading, writing, and drinking espresso.

Sherri Matthews grew up in her native England but in another life and for twenty years, she lived in California where she raised her three children. She has followed an eclectic career path in the medical and legal professions but writing has been her lifelong ambition. She started her blog, *A View From My Summerhouse*, in 2013 and writes a *Memoir Across the Pond* column at Carrot Ranch, an online literary community. Her work has appeared in various magazines and anthologies, is short-listed with *Fish Publishing* and received special mention at London's *Spread The Word Life Writing Prize*. Her memoir reached the finalist stage with *Page Turner Awards* and is listed in this year's *Cheshire Novel Prize*. While her memoir is out on submission, she is working on her next book and a poetry collection. Today she lives in England's West Country fulfilling her caregiving role with her family, including two black cats and a resident wild hedgehog, who successfully raised a family of hoglets in her garden during the UK's hottest summer on record in 2022.

Trent McDonald is originally from Ohio and now lives in New Hampshire, with a second home in Massachusetts, a small house near the shore of Swan Pond in Dennisport, where he enjoys kayaking, hiking, bicycling, and skiing. If "Computer Nerd" is a real occupation then we must consider Trent's "day job" as just that. His official title is currently "Systems Administrator" but he has worked in various aspects of computer science and IT over the years, which includes, web design, support, networking, mail administrator, programing, etc. When not plugging away at computers, Trent enjoys and participates in the arts. Music is in many ways the love of Trent's life. He plays the trumpet and keyboards, composing much of his own music. The visual arts are also important and as an avid photographer, Trent also draws and paints. Music might be the love of Trent's life but writing has been the core: living + thinking = writing. Trent has spent a good deal of time and energy getting his words down on paper, or the electrons on the screen.

Dr. Mike Martelli is a Health & Rehabilitation Neuropsychologist with 35 years of individualizing client strategies for Rebuilding Brains, Coping & Lives (Love, Work & Play) after Injury, Illness & Disease, Aging and all combinations, for patients and their families. Currently retired, Dr. Martelli has had a very active writing and speaking career, continues writing part-time and is contemplating a return to part-time work.

Mahesh Nair is an astute observer of people, culture, and human experience. He is the author of Chaotic Alleys: Collected Works, a fiction compilation of micro, flash, and short stories. He won the Strands International Flash Fiction Award, was shortlisted for Bath Flash Fiction Award and Micro Madness NFFD, was long-listed for the Reflex Fiction prize, and was highly commended at London Independent Story Prize. His work has appeared in Barren Magazine, Literary Orphans, The Bookends Review, Smokebox, Paragraph Planet, 101 Words, AdHoc Fiction, BlinkInk Print, and Crack the Spine, and has been featured in three anthologies. He was a contributing author for a CNF anthology, Lady by the River. He studied creative fiction writing at New York University.

Jeffrey D. Simmons is a native of Detroit, Michigan and currently resides in Houston, Texas. He retired from the United States Army, after 32 years of service as a Major, two combat tours in Afghanistan and Iraq, a bronze star, and several other awards. He earned a BA in Organizational Management and an MBA in Project Management both from Ashford University. Jeffrey's passion is service to others and veterans, which has motivated him to pursue a Ph.D. in Healthcare Administration. Jeff enjoys mentoring, volunteering, cooking, fishing, and writing. As a real-life role model, he manages his posttraumatic stress disorder (PTSD) one day at a time. and he is an inspirational American hero. He is the author of *Voices and Choices* and his personal blog is major1963.wordpress.com.

Robbie Cheadle is an award-winning, bestselling author who published thirteen children's book and three poetry books. Her work has also appeared in poetry and short story anthologies. Robbie also has two novels published under the name of Roberta Eaton Cheadle and has horror, paranormal, and fantasy short stories featured in several anthologies under this name. The ten *Sir Chocolate* children's picture books, co-authored by Robbie and Michael Cheadle, are written in sweet, short rhymes which are easy for young children to follow and are illustrated with pictures of delicious cakes and cake decorations. Each book also includes simple recipes or biscuit art directions which children can make under adult supervision. Robbie's blog includes recipes, fondant and cake artwork, poetry, and book reviews. https://robbiesinspiration.wordpress.com/

Mabel Kwong is a writer and lives in Melbourne, Australia. She has an MA in Communications with a focus on audience reception. Her writing explores cultural identities and the notion of belonging in a diverse world. Her work has appeared in academic journals, magazines, and online publications. She is an introvert, has an interest in astrology, and some of her time is spent reading and capturing moments through photography. She blogs regularly at www.mabelkwong.com.

Lauren Scott is a poet, fiction writer, and memoirist, and has shared her writing on baydreamerwrites.com for over ten years. She has authored two collections of poetry: *New Day, New Dreams* and *Finding a Balance.* Her memoir, *More than Coffee,* was published in 2021, and she is a contributing author to the anthology: *Poetry Treasures 2: Relationships* released in 2022. Her upcoming poetry collection, *Ever So Gently,* was released in June. Her work has been published on Spillwords Press where she was Author of the Month for May 2023. She lives in Northern California with her husband, Matt, of thirty-four years and their lab, Copper; they have two grown children. Her writing inspiration comes from her love of family, spending time in nature, and finding joy in the small things. Humor always finds its way into her life because without it, life would be colorless.

Cade Prior grew up in Richmond, Virginia, and discovered his passion for filmmaking at the age of 18. Six years later, he is an award-winning film director, editor, and cinematographer based in Austin, Texas. Cade produces mini-documentaries, a podcast, and personal YouTube content aimed at men in their 20s and 30s. In his free time, he enjoys reading, traveling, playing pickleball, and training jiu-jitsu. Keep an eye out for his upcoming book, "Intentionalism," set to release in early 2024.

Miriam Hurdle is a member of the Society of Children's Book Writers and Illustrators (SCBWI). Her publications include her poetry collection *Songs of Heartstrings,* her children's book, *Tina Lost in a Crowd,* and her memoir *The Winding Road.* Her poetry collection received the Solo "Medalist Winner" for the New Apple Summer eBook Award and achieved bestseller status on Amazon. Miriam earned a Doctor of Education from the University of La Verne in California. She retired after two years of rehabilitation counseling, fifteen years of public-school teaching, and ten years in school district administration. After living in Southern California for forty years, she and her husband moved to Portland, Oregon, to be close to her daughter, son-in-law, and granddaughters. When not writing, she engages in blogging, gardening, photography, and traveling. She blogs at https://theshowersofblessings.com

Marsha Ingrao, a retired teacher and educational consultant, now lives with her husband in Prescott, AZ. They have one pampered cat and enjoy traveling around Arizona and back to California to see friends and their son. Marsha's goal is to visit bloggers in the United States and around the world and to also visit National Parks in the Western US. Marsha enjoys blogging, writing, photography, and leading small groups in a local church.

Independently published with Priorhouse blog

Printed in Great Britain
by Amazon

35282461R00172